61-8445

3-14-62

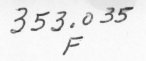
The View From The White House

A STUDY OF THE PRESIDENTIAL STATE OF THE UNION MESSAGES

Seymour H. Fersh

Public Affairs Press, Washington, D. C.

FOREWORD

Relationships between Congress and the President have long and rightly been a matter of concern and study for our political scientists. We know all too well that some of the most difficult political crises in the American experience have been occasioned by conflicts and impasses between the legislative and executive branches. As we look ahead to future decades and the challenges they hold for our political system, we can be sure that many of the severest tests of its adequacy will arise in the sector of Presidential-Congressional interaction.

Professor Seymour Fersh examines in this volume a principal facet of executive-legislative relations, the State of the Union Message. Thanks to his painstaking research, he is able to give us a full account of the historical development of the Message, how it responded to the shaping touches of Washington, Jefferson, Lincoln, Cleveland, Wilson, and our contemporary Presidents. Professor Fersh describes, with much insight, how the Union Message has become attuned to changing historical situations and forces, ranging from the Federalist monarchical milieu to Republican simplicity, from Lincolnian eloquence in the crucible of the Civil War to the ponderousness and quietude of the late nineteenth century, from the domestic social reforms of Wilson and the Roosevelts to America's position in the world today, a circumstance that brings Mr. Fersh to conclude that the "speech from the White House" is now concerned with the "state of the world" as well as of the union.

Some years ago, Charles A. Beard described the State of the Union Message as "the one great public document of the United States which is widely read and discussed." Mr. Fersh explains most satisfactorily why this has been so and, even more important, why it will remain so in the long future.

LOUIS W. KOENIG

New York City

TO HARRIETT,
DONALD, SUSAN, AND MARYL DEVI

PREFACE

Thirty-three men have sat in the presidential chair in the years from 1790 to 1960 and delivered a total of 170 annual messages. By making it a constitutional duty of the President "from time to time to give to the Congress information of the state of the Union, and recommend to their consideration such measures as he shall judge necessary and expedient," the founding fathers of the Republic succeeded in having placed before the lawmakers and the nation a continuous series of yearly assessments from the Chief Executive. No other governmental document has commanded the attention given to the annual message. It stands unchallenged, over the years, as front page copy. Newspapers have so treated it from the earliest days of the country and more recently, full radio and television coverage has been given whenever the President delivered his report in person.

The reasons for the sustained interest in the messages are clear. They have provided at least three important "views" from the White House: first, there is the view itself of unfolding events as seen from the nation's capital which is summarized by the President; second, there is the view or judgment of the President which the message represents; and third, there is the view of the presidency itself which is sometimes explicit and more often implicit in the manner with which the communication is delivered and the content which it contains.

The rewards held out to the reader of the annual message series are matched by the dangers involved. Each yearly report is best understood when considered within the frame-work of its own contemporary period—a cumulative length of time equal to United States history in its entirety. The requisite scholarship can be claimed by few and is not claimed by me. Furthermore, a history of the presidential documents is even more hazardous. One can not, after all, reasonably hope to accurately "map" in one readable volume a "territory" which consists of 170 messages ranging in length from 2,000 to 30,000 words each and totaling some two million. I do believe, however, that it is possible to chart with a degree of correctness the course which the "state of the Union" reports have followed in their development as an American political institution. The main focus of this study is on the changing function of the annual message.

Time and personality have worked their transformation on Article II, section 3 of the Constitution. "Information to Congress" has become information to the nation and to the world. "The state of the Union" has become the state of the Earth as well. While it is true that a President now has access to national and world audiences at a moment's notice, it is also true that his communication to Congress at its opening session will continue to be his most complete critique of the country's condition. The annual message gives promise of future service which will build on its honorable and useful past.

It is a pleasure to acknowledge my gratitude to three professors whose understanding of and feeling for American history nurtured my own affection for the subject: Dr. S. P. McCutchen, Dr. John C. Payne and Dr. Watt Stewart. Two other educators, my brothers Dr. Irving J. Fersh and Dr. George L. Fersh, carefully blazed the trail assisting and cheering me along. I am indebted to M. B. Schnapper of the Public Affairs Press, and to my friend Allan Angoff for expert editorial advice. My appreciation also goes to my parents and sisters; and to Anne and David Fein for their steadfast encouragement. Most of all, I am beholden to my dear wife and children who never lost faith that the project would be completed and who helped in every way to create the right atmosphere for study. Despite the help-mates, the book reveals shortcomings of which I am painfully aware. Under the rights of authorship I claim as my exclusive property all errors of commission and omission; whatever may be considered worthy of commendation I happily share with my large "joint family."

A grant from the College Development Fund of the Montclair State College, New Jersey helped to make this publication possible. For the vote of confidence which this award represents, I am grateful.

SEYMOUR H. FERSH

Upper Montclair, New Jersey

CONTENTS

Chapter One

PROLOGUE

Historians are people who record and interpret a narrative of events. In the United States this calling has in effect been undertaken by the Presidents on a yearly basis since 1790. It began when the framers of the Constitution made it a presidential duty to "give to Congress information of the state of the union, and recommend to their consideration such measures as he shall judge necessary and expedient." Of course, the Presidents are first and foremost chief executives and heads of political parties, not historians. This dual role has necessarily prejudiced the record; their main concern has been not with history "as it was" but more often with history as they hoped it was and would become.

When Article I of the Constitution directed Congress to meet on the first Monday, or soon after, in December of each year, it necessarily set the time for the delivery of the annual message. It became customary for the President, as soon as he had been notified that the lawmakers were ready to do business, to deliver his yearly report during the first days of the congressional session. Starting in 1934 the "state of the union" message has been given in January because of the twentieth amendment which moved up the convening date of Congress by eleven months.

The annual message has been the Presidents' chronicle. Its content abounds with grist for the professional historian's mill and is full of interest for the student of American affairs. All the "vital statistics" of a dynamic nation are paraded in yearly review in all but a few of the reports. The alternating concern of the Presidents with domestic and foreign affairs, and the proliferation of subject areas as the small country of four million moved to world prominence are recorded in the layers of message content. A few of the yearly reports set forth history-making doctrines, some announce precedent-breaking events, and all contribute to fuller comprehension of their times.

Understandably, few of the Presidents have interpreted exactly in the same way their duty "to report and recommend." While some have performed this task in personally delivered addresses, most have resorted to written messages. A few have avowed openly their intention of influencing Congress, the majority have endeavored carefully

1

to avoid any impression that they were "dictating" to the lawmakers. Some have been eloquent in their style; some have been painfully dull. A few have aimed their remarks at the vast audience beyond Capitol Hill, but most have been content merely to oblige Congress. Some saw a "state of the union" of many colors, harsh and bright; others reported it in a roseate setting. A handful of chief executives embraced their *duty* as they would a new bride, welcoming their responsibility as an opportunity; most accepted annual message time as they would an arranged marriage, with resignation and lackluster.

Regardless of how the Presidents have felt about the function of the annual message, it has continued to grow in importance, paralleling the growth of the United States and the federal government. In 1790 only the assembled Congress and a small number of guests heard Washington's address. In 1835 Jackson's message was considered so important that the *Cincinnati Commercial* spent two hundred dollars in order to get a copy of it within sixty hours.[1] A hundred years later historian Charles A. Beard wrote:

"Whatever may be its purport, the message is the one great public document of the United States which is widely read and discussed. Congressional debates receive scant notice, but the President's message is ordinarily printed in full in nearly every metropolitan daily, and is the subject of general editorial comment throughout the length and breadth of the land. It stirs the country; it often affects congressional elections; and it may establish grand policy."[2]

Today television permits millions of Americans to "sit in" with Congress and millions more throughout the world hear and read the President's report. The "speech from the White House" is now concerned with the "state of the world" as well as of the union; the two have become inseparable. Along with the United States itself, the annual message has moved into the center of the world arena.

In commenting on the origin of the "state of the union" message, scholars have called attention to its similarity to political practice in Great Britain. In his book on sources of the Constitution C. Ellis Stevens emphasizes that "the President's message is derived from the royal act of communicating with parliament."[3] Concerning Washington's first annual address James Hart states that "the analogy to the speech from the throne and the address in reply in the British monarchy is unmistakable."[4] In England the custom has been for the reigning monarch to make an address at the opening of parliament. The message is prepared by the prime minister and his cabinet and is in fact a legislative program for the coming year. It usually includes a review of action taken by the executive, a list of measures to be introduced in parliament, and a general summary of subject areas confronting the nation. After the king (or queen) delivers the address, both houses hear a rereading of the message and then formulate and vote on replies to the speech.[5]

The resemblance of the presidential annual message to the king's address in parliament is clear but it is a serious over simplification to infer that the duty placed on the President was patterned directly on the English system. Overt borrowing from British precedent was highly unpopular in the 1780s. Indeed, the framers often specifically disclaimed that there had been any derivation of the Constitution from non-American sources. They insisted that practically every feature of the document had been suggested by colonial and state experience.[6] Of course, the early American governments themselves were saturated with British customs and precedents.

When the founding fathers sought to create an executive who could deal effectively with national problems, the search for a model led to New York state because only there had the governor escaped "complete subordination" to the legislature.[7] The New York Constitution of 1777 became the source for many of the clauses in the federal Constitution dealing with presidential duties. This is especially true of the clause calling for information to Congress; its origin can be traced directly to article XIX of the New York document which provided "it shall be the duty of the governor to inform the legislature, at every session, of the condition of the State, so far as may respect his department: to recommend such matters to their consideration as shall appear to him to concern its good government, welfare and prosperity. . . ."[8]

This article had been brought to the attention of the constitutional convention at Philadelphia by Charles Pinckney of South Carolina. His plan drew heavily from New York's charter and provided, for example, that it shall be a duty of the President "to inform the Legislature at every session of the condition of the United States, so far as may respect his Department—to recommend Matters to their Consideration such as shall appear to him to concern their good government, welfare and prosperity."[9] The Virginia plan, submitted to the convention on the same day as Pinckney's, became the basis for considerable discussion, amendments and additions. On July 26th the committee of detail was given the Virginia plan (now enlarged to twenty-five general resolutions) as well as the New Jersey and Pinckney plans. It was asked to draft a workable constitution and report back ten days later. At this point the resolution in the Virginia plan pertaining to the presidency contained the provision that "there should be a single executive with power to execute the national laws, to veto acts of the national legislature, and to appoint offices in cases not otherwise provided for, and who should be removable by impeachment."[10] There was no mention of a duty "to report and recommend." James Wilson, a member of the detail committee, grafted phraseology from the Pinckney plan onto the Virginia resolutions with the result that the committee report on August 6th contained article X, section 2: "He [the President] shall, from time to time, give information to the Legislature, of the state of the Union: he may recommend to their consideration such measures as he shall judge necessary, and expedient."[11]

The proposed constitution was debated article by article, section by section, clause by clause. When section 2 of article X came before the delegates on August 24th a series of motions changed the wording:

"On the question to transpose the word 'information' and to insert it after the word 'legislature' in the first clause of 2 sect. 10 article it passed in the affirmative."

"It was moved and seconded to strike out the words 'he may' and to insert the word 'and' before the word 'recommend' in the second clause of the 2 sect. 10 article which passed in the affirmative."[12]

No record of individual voting on these two motions was reported. *Madison's Journal* states that it was on the insistence of Gouverneur Morris that "he may" was struck out, and "and" inserted before "recommend" so as, according to Morris, "to make it the *duty* of the President to recommend, and thence prevent umbrage or cavil at his doing it."[13]

Debate on the draft proposals of the committee of detail was completed on September 10th and the proceedings of the convention were referred to the committee of style and arrangements. The latter transposed section 2 of article X into section 3 of article II, changed one word, altered the punctuation, and decapitalized one word. On September 17th the delegates signed the engrossed copy of the Constitution. In final form section 3 of article II read: "He [the President] shall from time to time give to the Congress Information of the State of the Union, and recommend to their Consideration such Measures as he shall judge necessary and expedient; . . ."

New York had not only inspired the "letter" of the presidential duty to "report and recommend;" it also provided a good example of the "spirit" in which the executive responsibility should be carried out.

In that state the first speech of the royal governor to the legislature is traced back to 1692.[14] The ceremonial followed custom in England where by the time of Henry VIII it was fixed political practice for the king to deliver an address at the opening of parliament.[15] As reported in the journals of New York's colonial council and assembly, the procedure was for the governor to receive permission from the speaker and then address the legislature recommending such measures as he thought appropriate. A copy of the speech was then entered in the official records. Formal debate of the message followed in each chamber after which replies were drafted and presented in person to the chief executive. When De Witt Clinton became New York's first governor under the state constitution of 1777 he continued the colonial practice.[16] On the day of his initial message ancient royal ceremonials were everywhere in evidence. After the Assembly was organized a committee of two members was deputized to inform him that "the Houses are ready to proceed to business, and wait His Excellency's commands." Clinton said that "he would send for the House immediately." That afternoon the governor's private secretary appeared in the Assembly and announced that "His Excellency requires the immediate attendance of the House in the court room." The Assemblymen went to the court room, heard the governor's address, and returned to their own chamber. The Speaker reported that "His Excellency had been pleased to make a speech to the House, and to present him a copy thereof." The message was read and entered in the *Journal*.[17]

The severing of political ties between the New and the Old World had been clean cut; not so were the ties of traditions and customs which had passed *cum lacte*, with the mother's milk. The new nation might loudly assert its independence from Great Britain but many of its political practices and ceremonials were to have a "Made in England" look.

By August 6, 1788, eleven states having ratified the Constitution, Congress took steps to place it into effect. The government was formed at the federal capital in New York City and life was breathed into the still form of the untried charter. The prologue was over.

Chapter Two

FEDERALIST POMP AND REPUBLICAN SIMPLICITY

In New York City on April 30, 1789, George Washington took the oath as first President of the United States. Following the swearing-in ceremony he delivered the first inaugural address, citing section 3 of article II as the constitutional basis:

"By the article establishing the executive department it is made the duty of the President 'to recommend to your consideration such measures as he shall judge necessary and expedient.' The circumstances under which I now meet you will acquit me from entering into that subject further than to refer to the great constitutional charter under which you are assembled, and which, in defining your powers, designated the objects to which your attention is to be given. It will be more consistent with those circumstances, and far more congenial with the feelings which actuate me, to substitute, in place of recommendation of particular measures, the tribute that is due to the talents, rectitude, and the patriotism which adorn the characters selected to devise and adopt them."[1]

Directed formally to "Fellow-Citizens of the Senate and House of Representatives," the speech concerned itself mainly with expressions of appreciation, confidence in the future, and devout wishes for providential favor. After the address, the legislators joined Washington at church services and returned later to their respective chambers to consider what action to take regarding the message. In the House, it was quickly decided to follow parliamentary and state custom by presenting a reply to the President in response to his address. James Madison was appointed to head the committee authorized to draft a reply and report back to the Congressmen.[2]

The Senate, however, was the scene of lively debate warning against too many British-inspired precedents. Even before the inaugural ceremony, there had been much wrangling. Vice President John Adams had been concerned as to how the inaugural address should be treated. "How shall I behave? How shall we receive it? Shall it be standing or sitting?" he asked the Senators.[3] When one of them referred to practice in the House of Commons, another commented that he thought the rules in Great Britain to be of no consequence to them. But no Senator objected when a member from New York proclaimed, "Long live George Washington"—an obvious derivative of the familiar monarchial "Long live the King." When Adams, after the inaugural, referred to the President's address as "his most gracious speech," he evoked from Senator William Maclay a motion to strike the words from the Senate minutes:

"We have lately had a hard struggle for our liberty against kingly authority. The minds of men are still heated; everything related to that species of government is odious to the people. The words prefixed to the President's speech are the same that are usually placed before the Speech of his Britannic Majesty. I know they will give offense. I consider them as improper."[4]

Richard Henry Lee supported Maclay and the expression "most gracious speech" was struck out—an indication that procedure based on colonial traditions would have to make allowance for resentment toward certain features of those traditions.

There was further delay in delivering the replies to the President when the two chambers were unable to agree on a suitable title with which to address the chief executive. The Senate's "His highness, the President of the United States of America and Protector of their Liberties" was unacceptable to the House. Representative Thomas Tucker of South Carolina voiced majority opinion: "Does the dignity of a nation consist in the distance between the first magistrate and its citizens? Does it consist in the exaltation of one man, and the humiliation of the rest? If so, the most despotic government is the most dignified."[5]

"For my part," James Madison replied later, ". . . I do not conceive titles to be so pregnant with danger as some gentlemen apprehend. I believe a President of the United States, clothed with all the powers given in the Constitution would not be a dangerous person to the liberties of America, if you were to load him down with all the titles of Europe and Asia."[6] The controversy was settled by agreement to use "To the President of the United States" without addition of titles. With this hurdle cleared, the House members met with Washington at his residence on May 8th and the Senators called on him ten days later, both groups to thank him for his inaugural address and to receive his short reply of gratitude.

For the remainder of the congressional session, Washington relied almost exclusively on written messages to communicate with Congress. The lawmakers recessed in September and when they reconvened on the first Monday of January, 1790, Washington notified the presiding officers that he had some information to transmit orally and wished to know when and where Congress would receive him. Three days later committees from both Houses went to the President, announced that Congress was organized and would receive his communication in the Senate chamber at his convenience. Washington chose the next morning at eleven o'clock.[7]

This initiatory step taken by the President and acquiesced in by Congress marked the beginning of the annual message series. The constitutional mandate was the same one cited by Washington when he delivered his inaugural address: the duty placed on the President to give information and make recommendations to Congress. All preparations made, Washington went in ceremonial state to deliver his message. His diary presents a detailed picture of his reception on that historic January 8, 1790:

"According to appointment, at 11 o'clock, I set out for the City Hall in my coach, preceded by Colonel Humphreys and Majr. Jackson in uniform (on my two white horses) and followed by Messrs. Lear and Nelson, in my chariot, and Mr. Lewis, on horseback, following them. In their rear was the Chief Justice of the United States and Secretary of the Treasury and War Departments, . . . At the outer door of the hall I was met by the door-keepers of the Senate and House, conducted to the door of the Senate Chamber; and passing from thence . . . I took my seat. The gentlemen who attended me followed and took their stand behind the Senators; the whole rising as I entered. After being seated, at which time the members of both Houses also sat, I rose (as they also did) and made my speech; delivering one copy to the President of the Senate, and another to the Speaker of the Houses of Representatives—after which, and being a few moments seated, I retired, bowing on each side to the assembly (who stood) as I passed, and descending to the lower hall, attended as before, I returned with them to my house."[8]

At the next session of the First Congress meeting the same year for the first time in Philadelphia, Washington again delivered his annual message in person. It was customary for the public to be admitted and as many as could be accommodated heard the speech. Except for the change to the more spacious House chamber for the address in 1793, Washington followed the same course in all of his appearances before Congress. James Bryce's comment is both accurate and picturesque: "Washington used to deliver his address orally, like an English king, and drove in a coach and six to open Congress with something of an English king's state."[9] The parallel with British custom was obvious. In a chapter pointedly entitled "An

Imitation of Court" Henry J. Ford writes that Washington was following very closely the precedents derived from the English system under which he had been educated.[10]

This predilection for pomp was consistent with Washington's concept of the presidency which has been likened to that of a constitutional monarch before the days of responsible ministers.[11] Edward S. Corwin rates the office under Washington and John Adams as "quasi-monarchical" in comparison to its "ultra-Whig" character under Jefferson.[12]

The constitutional duty to make recommendations was approached gingerly. Washington did not interpret it as giving him the right to initiate specific legislation. To have done so at this time would have been considered an encroachment on the lawmaking prerogatives assigned to Congress under the separation of powers doctrine. He restricted himself to a general enumeration of the subject areas which he thought needed congressional attention and this done, he relied on the legislators to take appropriate action. His remark in 1793— after reporting on presidential action concerning prize ships—was typical: "It rests with the wisdom of Congress to correct, improve, or enforce this plan of procedure."[13]

However, Washington's prestige gave weight to his recommendations even when voiced in a deferential way. Consequently some of his cabinet officials, Hamilton in particular, sought to have their views incorporated in the annual message because this inclusion would enhance their liklihood of being enacted into law. The President helped the process by soliciting suggestions; a letter to Hamilton in 1790 requested information which could be used in the annual message of that year: "We are approaching the first Monday in December by hasty strides. I pray you, therefore, to revolve in your mind such measures as may be proper for me to lay before Congress, not only in your own department, (if there be any) but such others of a general nature, as may happen to occur to you, that I may be prepared to open the session with such communications, as shall appear to merit attention."[14]

The oral form of the Washington annual messages placed practical limitations on their length. The President could either survey many areas in a rather superficial way or he could focus on a few main issues and give them a detailed treatment. Washington favored the compendium approach although on occasion he departed from this formula as in 1794 when he gave over almost all of the message to a comprehensive report on the Whisky Rebellion and action that had been taken by the executive branch. The general pattern of his eight messages was to commence with greetings and religious thanksgiving and then skim over the contemporary scene, devoting brief paragraphs to the examination of a variety of subjects. Washington did not go into details, convinced as he was that his main function was to bring a number of issues to the attention of the lawmakers leaving the specific working out of legislation to them. His concluding remarks were directed to each chamber separately, addressing matters dealing with taxation and debt to members of the House of Representatives. On the occasion of his first annual address he initiated the practice of sending along reports from cabinet officers to supplement the message, explaining: "I have directed the proper officers to lay before you, respectively, such papers and estimates as regards the affairs particularly recommended to your consideration, and necessary to convey to you that information of the state of the Union which it is my duty to afford."[15]

The last paragraph of the Washington annual mesages almost invariably contained a pledge by the President to work with Congress for the good of the country: "the great object to which our cares and efforts ought to be directed" and one from which he derived great satisfaction "in the pleasing though arduous task of insuring to our fellow-citizens the blessings which they have a right to expect from a free, efficient, and equal government." He favored a formal, reserved style of presentation which was felt to be appropriate for the high ceremony of the occasion. A note of humility and sense of duty was ever present. The opening remarks of the first message of his second term are characteristic:

"Since the commencement of the term for which I have been again called into office no fit occasion has arisen for expressing to my fellow-citizens at large the deep and respectful sense which I feel of the renewed testimony of public approbation. While on the one hand it awakened my gratitude for all those instances of affectionate partiality with which I have been honored by my country, on the other hand it could not prevent an earnest wish for that retirement from which no private consideration should ever have torn me. But influenced by the belief that my conduct would be estimated according to its real motives, and that the people, and the authorities derived from them, would support exertions having nothing personal for their object, I have obeyed the suffrage which commanded me to resume the Executive power; and I humbly implore that Being on whose

will the fate of nations depends to crown with success our mu
endeavors for the general happiness."[16]

The disposition of the Presidents to report contemporary events
with confidence and optimism—a trademark of the annual messages
until 1900—had its origin with Washington. This "bullish" attitude
was usually reflected throughout the entire message and often was
specifically given voice in a paragraph which congratulated Congress
on the "favorable prospects which continue to distinguish our public
affairs." Exceptions intruded during the Washington administration
in 1792 when threatening Indian hostilities were reported on the
Northwest frontier, and in 1794 when the Whisky Rebellion caused
the President to admit of some apprehension. By 1795, however, he
felt better: "I trust I do not deceive myself when I indulge in the
persuasion that I have never met you at any period when more
than at the present the situation of our public affairs has afforded
just cause for mutual congratulations."[17] Associated with this sanguine
reporting was almost perennial lavish religious thanksgiving, such as
the concluding paragraph of the 1794 address:

"Let us unite, therefore, in imploring the Supreme Ruler of Nations
to spread his holy protection over these United States; to turn the
mechinations of the wicked to the confirming of our Constitution;
to enable us at all times to root out internal sedition and put invasion
to flight; to perpetuate to our country that prosperity which His
goodness has already conferred, and to verify the anticipation of this
Government being a safeguard to human rights."[18]

The annual address was accepted as a logical and permissable way
for the President to acquit himself of his duty to report to Congress
but the reply to the address became the focus of continuing debate
in the first ten years of the Republic. Written by a special committee
in each House, the "address in reply" was debated by the entire
membership and the approved version was read to the President at
his house usually within a week after the presidential speech. A few
hundred words in length, the reply uniformly repeated the recommendations made by the President—almost word for word—and
pledged the co-operation of each House. The style was formal and
the tone respectful. The chief executive, in his turn, was equally
gracious in thanking the lawmakers for their remarks and promise
of support. During the Washington and John Adams administrations
Congress outdid even the British in showing deference to its President. All of its members trooped to his residence to share in the

replies whereas representatives in parliament waited in person upon the king rarely, only on very special occasions. In colonial and state practice replies to the governors were presented through committees.[19] Senator William Maclay denounced the business as a "stale ministerial trick in Britain, to get the Houses of Parliament to chime in with the speech, and then consider them as pledged to suport any measure which could be grafted on the speech."[20]

The inauguration of the new government in 1789 had been accepted as an unique and momentous event and so, when after Washington's inaugural address, Congress voted to deliver a reply, opposition was restrained even though the procedure followed British practice. When in 1790 the Federalists insisted on keeping the reply as a permanent part of the annual message ceremony, the Anti-Federalists began immediately to agitate for its abolition. There was a rising tide of protest against pomp associated with monarchy and aristocracy. The ritual of "echoing speeches" was singled out for special attack by many Republican newspapers. "Is this really a law?" one editor asked. "Is it a congressional precedent? The Nation will soon be as abject, as grovelling as the meanest oriental alive. . . . Future and perhaps rapacious Presidents may be the dark and despotic Caesars of America. . . . Is it the duty of Congress, are they in conscience bound to endanger the political system by paying compliments?"[21] Long debates ensued in Congress over the words to be used in the replies and the practice itself was under constant criticism. To meet the many objections the content of the answers to the President became more general and its tone became less cordial. In 1796 the replies to Washington's final annual address were especially laudatory only because of his approaching retirement from office but the tribute was not without its critics. One Congressman insisted that the reply ought not "to carry our expressions beyond the bounds of moderation" and that it should "adhere to the truth."[22]

From 1790 to 1796 the annual message content revealed a young nation faced with serious problems of organization and survival. In his first yearly report Washington noted the accession of North Carolina to the union, reported Indian hostilities, and congratulated the country on its rising credit and respectability. He suggested to Congress that "among the many interesting objects which will engage your attention" should be concern with common defense, a uniform rule of naturalization, uniformity in currency, weights, and measures; advancement of agriculture, commerce and manufacturing; facilitation of "intercourse between the distant parts of our country by due attention to the post-office and post-roads," and the establishment of a national university. In support of a militia and home manufacture of military supplies, Washington insisted that "To be prepared for war is one of the most effectual means of preserving peace." In calling for patronage of science and literature, he pointed out that "Knowledge is in every country the surest basis of public happiness. In one in which the measures of government received their impressions so immediately from the sense of the community as ours it is proportionably essential." His succeeding messages recorded national "first steps": subscriptions to the Bank of the United States, taxes on distilled spirits, designation of a district ten miles square for the permanent seat of government, a census report of a 4,000,000 population, and the recommendation that a military academy be established. Congress was urged to reduce the national debt as quickly as possible— a request which was much reiterated by succeeding Presidents.

In 1791 Washington spoke of the "disturbed situation of Europe" and warned that "we should not overlook the tendency of a war." Two years later with most of the European nations at war with France he stressed defense preparations:

"The United States ought not to indulge in a persuasion that, contrary to the order of human events, they will forever keep at a distance those painful appeals to arms with which the history of every other country abounds. There is a rank due to the United States among nations which will be withheld, if not absolutely lost, by the reputation of weakness. If we desire to avoid insult, we must be able to repel it; if we desire to secure peace, one of the most powerful instruments of our rising prosperity, it must be known that we are at all times ready for war."[23]

Under increasing censure by the Anti-Federalists for his Administration, Washington explained in 1794 that "my policy in our foreign transactions has been to cultivate peace with all the world; to observe treaties with pure and absolute faith; to check every deviation from the line of impartiality; to explain what may have been misapprehended and correct what may have been injurious to any nation, and having thus acquired the right, to lose no time in acquiring the ability to insist upon justice being done to ourselves."[24]

When John Adams took office in 1797 he understood fully that he had not likewise taken possession of the prestige and esteem which had been Washington's. Although he continued the "monarchical" ceremony of delivering the address in person, he was obviously less sure of his position. Adams was more the reporter and less the recommender. Aware of powerful opposition in Congress to many of his policies, he frequently showed a willingness to placate the lawmakers. A passage from his 1799 message is characteristic: "As to myself, it is my anxious desire to execute the trust reposed in me as to render the people of the United States prosperous and happy. I rely with entire confidence on your cooperation in objects equally your care, and that our mutual labors will serve to increase and confirm union among our fellow-citizens and an unshaken attachment to our government."[25]

Adams' election had been the signal for renewed assaults by the Republicans on all vestiges of royal ceremonials. The annual address and reply were seized upon for special rigorous flayings. Congress continued to draft and deliver "echoing speeches" to the President but the replies became increasingly less commital and less cordial.

The inclination to see the "state of the union" in its more pleasing hues found favor with Adams and his expressions of religious thanksgiving went beyond any other President in assigning to Providence an active role in the affairs of the United States. "Bad news" when reported was accepted with "reverence and resignation" as in 1798 when Adams referred to the "dispensations of Divine Providence in the alarming and destructive pestilence" which was then afflicting Philadelphia.

War was imminent in Europe when Adams became President and his annual messages gave much attention to foreign affairs—an indication that the "splendid historic isolation" traditionally ascribed to early American history was not a reality in his time. In 1797 he observed: "Connected with some by treaties and with all by commerce, no important event there [Europe] can be indifferent to us."[26] Regarding the home front, Adams speaking in 1800 in the Senate chamber of the new Capitol congratulated Congress "on the prospect of a residence not to be changed." The presidential election of that year marked the end of Federalist reign and Adams cautioned against extremes which might result from the "revolution of 1800."

Speaking as an elder statesman in what was in effect his farewell address, Adams counseled: "If [in the United States] we find reason to rejoice at the prospect which presents itself; if we perceive the interior of our country prosperous, free, and happy; if all enjoy in safety, under the protection of laws emanating only from the general will, the fruits of their own labor, we ought to fortify and cling to those institutions which have been the source of such real felicity and resist with unabating perseverance the progress of those dangerous innovations which may diminish their influence."[27]

When the Democratic-Republican party won the presidency in 1801 it sought to implement its belief that leadership should be exercised by Congress not by the President.   Thomas Jefferson believed that there was danger to a democratic system where the chief executive held broad and discretionary powers; his concept of a limited executive was "more Whig than that of the British Whigs themselves in subordinating it to the 'supreme legislative power'."[28]   However, through the use of the party caucus and floor leaders enforcing discipline, Jefferson was able to push many of his policies into law. It was from his position as party leader, rather than as President, that he exercised influence.   John Marshall's prediction that Jefferson would weaken the presidency but increase his personal power through party organization proved to be fundamentally correct.

In keeping with his election promise of a return to "simple republican forms of government" and in consonance with the concept of minimizing presidential prerogatives, Jefferson announced that he would communicate with Congress at annual message time by a written document which would require no reply.   The break with tradition was dramatic and decisive.   His private secretary, unescorted, brought the message to Congress and handed identical copies to the presiding officer of each House.   No more would the President arrive in an ornamental coach-and-six with military escort to address a congressional assemblage decked out in full dress of powdered hair, satin coats, knee-breeches, and silver buckled slippers.[29]

In identical letters to the Speaker and the Vice President, Jefferson explained his reasons for not appearing in person to address the first session of the Seventh Congress:

"The circumstances under which we find ourselves at this place rendering inconvenient the mode heretofore practiced of making by personal address the first communication between the legislative and executive branches, I have adopted that by message, as used in all subsequent occasions through the session.   In doing this I have had principal regard to the convenience of the legislature, to the economy of their time, to their relief from the embarrassment of immediate answers on subjects not yet fully before them, and to the benefits thence resulting to the public affairs.   Trusting that a procedure founded in these motives will meet their approbation, I beg leave

through you, sir, to communicate the inclosed message, with the documents accompanying it, to the honorable the Senate, and pray you
accept for yourself and them the homage of my high respect and
consideration."[80]

Scholars have not agreed as to the order of importance of the
factors which persuaded Jefferson to replace the oral address with
a written message. Charles Warren cites the strong political objections which existed among the Democratic-Republicans to the address
and reply, and adds (at the suggestion of Henry Cabot Lodge) that
"Jefferson was a poor speaker and consequently disliked to make
speeches."[81] Woodrow Wilson, in 1889, and William Howard Taft,
in 1916, both over simplified the motive by emphasizing Jefferson's
"lack of pleasure or facility in public speaking."[82] Edward S. Corwin
suggests a combination of causes; there was indeed so much opposition to the continuation of the presidential address that "when the
government moved to the new capital on the Potomac, and it was
found that Pennsylvania Avenue was no better than a quagmire
which it was dangerous to life and limb to traverse by carriage,
Jefferson, who was well aware that he wrote much better than he
spoke, decided to replace 'the speech from the Throne,' as his partisans
termed it, with a message sent by messenger."[83]

Norman Small charges that Jefferson, "having neither the renown
of his predecessor nor an inclination for public speaking," was not
being completely candid when, disregarding this deficiency, he argued
that the presidential address "smacked of Royal England" and in-
timated "that its continued observance would inevitably result in
the undesirable domination of the Legislature by a vigorous Executive."[84] But Henry Adams insisted, most correctly, that Jefferson's
political philosophy and the policy of the new Democratic-Republican
party was the context within which abandonment of the address
should be assessed. In theory at least, the executive now was to
receive his instructions from the legislators. While Jefferson did not
assign political reasons for not appearing before Congress, Henry
Adams stressed that the ceremonial itself was clearly a political
issue.[85] The President did give his inaugural address in person which
indicates that he saw a distinction between the occasion of being
sworn-in and of the opening of Congress. Jefferson's personal inclination to avoid what he called "aristocratic foppery," and his
apparent disinclination toward public speaking were most likely
contributing but not controlling factors in his precedent-breaking
action. The importance of the political element may be inferred

from the rash of outbreaks which came from Federalists and traditionalists.

One Boston editor held Jefferson's action to be "highly disrespectful to the Legislature . . . an humble imitation of the mode in which Bonaparte communicated to the French Legislature."[36] A New Hampshire newspaper commented sarcastically that "Mr. Jefferson is an original genius—the inventor of Messages," and it continued caustically that any change from the practices of Washington and Adams was enough to justify the new mode to Republicans. The *Washington Federalist* saw the innovation as 'intended to catch some childish applause" and deplored the fact that the message 'was not sent to the House in his [Jefferson's] own handwriting, hence we presume it was laboriously revised before submitted to public inspection." The *Gazette of the United States* likened Jefferson to an "Eastern prince" who remained in his palace out of sight of the people, communicating with them by messenger. The editorial concluded, "It is but reasonable to suppose that the people's representatives will feel self-respect to omit to wait upon him with an Answer."

The controversy was enlivened by sharp retorts in defense of the President. The *National Aegis* argued: "The parade and pageantry of a personal attendance upon the Legislature may afford to a monarch an opportunity for displaying his sacred person to the gazing eyes of the populace, but in a government like ours when a President may be seen and heard without a formal exhibition of his person, there can be no occasion for this splendid raree-show."

Observing that "the spirit of faction must be drained to the dregs when there is nothing to be said against the President but that his communication to Congress has been in the form of a message rather than in that of a speech," the *Independent Chronicle* insisted that the address and reply were a waste of time and money.

Attack and counter-attack were more a reflection of partisan politics than of a basic difference of opinion regarding the new mode of message delivery. Significantly, the written communication obviated the need for a congressional response and it was, after all, the reply which had engendered the greatest amount of discord in Congress. There was widespread feeling on both sides of the aisle that much acrimonious and futile debate could now be avoided. Jefferson wrote to a friend on December 20, 1801 that, "Our winter campaign has opened with more good humor than I expected" because "by sending a Message, instead of making a Speech at the opening of the session, I have prevented the bloody conflict to which the making of an Answer would have committed them. They consequently were able to set into real business at once, without losing 10 or 12 days in combatting an answer."[37]

Even Jefferson's salutation—"Fellow-Citizens of the Senate and House of Representatives"—caused consternation among Federalist forces. John Adams had been wont to greet Congress with "Gentlemen of the Senate and Gentlemen of the House of Representatives." The *Gazette of the United States* promptly accused Jefferson of copying the French style of address: "He might have spared the insult to the feelings of some of the members by saying 'Gentlemen and Fellow Citizens' and then he properly would have included all the members." This indictment was either ignorant or unmindful of Washington's consistent use of the same greeting then used by Jefferson. In each of his seven succeeding annual messages he prefaced his report with the simple designation: "To the Senate and House of Representatives of the United States."

Jefferson's annual messages read like professorial sermons on urgent national questions set in philosophic perspective without specific solutions. The manner was that of a senior statesman offering universalized good advice rather than that of a chief executive initiating policy. From his first message onward, he carefully refrained from any appearance that he sought to dominate Congress. Recommendations of specific legislation were studiously avoided. He was satisfied to sketch his position in a generalized way with statements of principle:

"That all should be satisfied with any order of things is not to be expected; but I indulge the pleasing persuasion that the great body of our citizens will cordially concur in honest and disinterested efforts which have for their object to preserve the General and State Governments in their constitutional form and equilibrium; to maintain peace abroad, and order and obedience to the laws at home; to establish principles and practices of administration favorable to the security of liberty and property, and to reduce expenses to what is necessary for the useful purposes of Government."[38]

The tenor of all his messages was consistently friendly in tone and conciliatory in nature. The concluding sentiments expressed in his 1801 communication were typical: "Nothing shall be wanting on my part to inform as far as in my power the legislative body, nor to carry that judgment into faithful execution."

The introduction of the written message opened the door to changes in content. Under Washington and Adams there had been an attempt within the constraints of an oral address to give an over-all picture of the contemporary "state of the union." The message had been of necessity general and superficial in its accounting. With the switch to a written version a more detailed report was now possible. The internal organization of Jefferson's annual messages, however, did not change perceptibly. Like his predecessors he devoted the initial paragraphs to general observations, reserved the main body of the message for reporting and recommending, and used the concluding sections for pledges of friendly co-operation with Congress and to offer religious thanksgiving for the nation's manifold blessings. Jefferson discontinued the practice of directing specific parts to either of the Houses—an example which has been followed by all succeeding Presidents. His written communications averaged little more in length than had the previous oral ones; his first annual message was his longest and its 3,000 words was about the same length as the wordiest Washington one.

In his first inaugural address, Jefferson conveniently summarized a program which he hoped to enact: economy in the national government, a strict interpretation of the Constitution, support of states' rights, guardianship of civil liberties, facilitation of majority rule, and promotion of "peace, commerce, and honest friendship with all nations, entangling alliances with none." His first annual message recommended that all excise taxes be repealed: "War, indeed, and untoward events may change this prospect of things . . . but sound principles will not justify our taxing the industry of our fellow-citizens to accumulate treasure for wars to happen we know not when, and which might not, perhaps, happen but from the temptations offered by that treasury."

The "states rights" doctrine received Jefferson's full endorsement: "When we consider that this Government is charged with the external and mutual relations only of these States; that the States themselves have principal care of our persons, our property, and our reputation, constituting the great field of human concerns, we may well doubt whether our organization is not too complicated, too expensive; whether offices and officers have not been multiplied unnecessarily and sometimes injuriously to the service they were meant to promote."[39]

However, Jefferson's yearly reports reveal that the pressure of circumstances turned him from the course which he had so sanguinely laid out. By 1805 his message told of "violence and wrong" suffered at the hands of the Spanish and Barbary Coast powers, and of disrespect to American rights from England and France. Preparation for war was advised; a negation of his neutrality plea made in 1803.[40] The *Chesapeake* affair in which a British boarding party captured the ship, and "some fermentation" among the Indians caused further presidential concern in 1807.

When not enmeshed in foreign affairs, Jefferson seemed pleased to dwell at length on domestic developments. He reported in detail the explorations of Lewis and Clark to the northwest, the expeditions of Freeman on the Red River, and Pike's journey to the source of the Mississippi. A noteworthy entry was Jefferson's reminder to Congress in 1806 to prepare legislation to end the African slave trade: "Although no law you may pass can take prohibitory effect till the first day of the year 1808, yet the intervening period is not too long to prevent by timely notice expeditions which can not be completed before that day."[41] The beginnings of a national policy were indicated in the President's support of an internal improvements program. He argued in 1806 that revenue from the tariff on foreign produced luxuries should be used for public education, roads, canals, and other betterments. His caution that this could be done only after a constitutional amendment did not hide the fact that the party in power did not fear the extension of federal controls as much as it had when out of office. Jefferson's position continued to broaden; in 1808 he expressed the hope that any surplus treasury money would be applied to internal improvements, adding that some action might be possible "under the powers which Congress may already possess." Even the acceptance of a permanent condition whereby the United States did its own manufacturing received his sanction in his final message.

The extent to which Jefferson's incumbency in the presidential chair had dulled his pre-election scruples about discretionary chief executives is indicated by his explanation of action taken to secure military supplies in 1807: "To have awaited a previous and special sanction by law would have lost occasions which might not be retrieved. I did not hesitate, therefore, to authorize engagements for such supplements . . . as would render it adequate to the emergencies threatening us, and I trust that the Legislature, feeling the same anxiety for the safety of our country, so materially advanced by this precaution, will approve, when done, what they would have seen so important to be done if then assembled."[42]

James Madison, James Monroe, and John Quincy Adams inherited the Jeffersonian principle which championed primacy for representative assemblies but lacking the personal and party stature of a Jefferson, leadership passed in fact as well as in theory to Congress. The Presidents owed their election more to the party caucus than to the public and they were not disposed to risk a break with the lawmakers. The presidential office had indeed been weakened. In the hands of circumspect chief executives, the annual message carried a blurred and self-effacing imprint. Factual reporting more and more crowded out recommendations, policy proposals, general observations. A detailed treasury report became a fixed feature. The Presidents threw a wider net in search of materials for their report, bringing Congress a greater catch in variety and multitude. The resulting dish, however, often proved unsorted and unpalatable to all but the most avid customer. In short, the annual message became more itemized and more dull; longer and less read by the public—more like a lantern hanging from the stern of the Ship of State than like a searchlight scanning the unlit course ahead.

The contemporary presidential philosophy regarding the function of the annual message was characteristically put by Monroe in 1821:

"In this annual communication . . . the whole scope of our political concerns naturally comes into view, that errors, if such have been committed, may be corrected; that defects which have become manifest may be remedied; and, on the other hand, that measures which were adopted on due deliberation, and which experience has shown are just in themselves . . . should be persevered in and supported. In performing this necessary and very important duty I shall endeavor to place before you on its merits every subject that is thought to be entitled to your particular attention in as distinct and clear a light as I may be able."[48]

The message style became flat and perfunctory. The text lost its eloquence, warmth, and personality. Only the first and last paragraphs which were reserved for greetings, pledges of co-operation and religious thanksgiving retained some semblance of rhetoric. The "scissors and paste" message which depended for its bulk on summations of departmental reports began with Madison and continued to grow longer and longer with few exceptions into the second decade of the twentieth century. Four of Madison's annual messages exceeded 3,000 words each. Monroe confirmed the trend when all of his contained more than 4,000 words each with the exception of the one in 1820 and his final message went over 7,500. In 1825

Adams used 8,000 words and although his next three messages were shorter, none were less than 6,000. The Presidents were succumbing to the writer's ancient curse of over-writing and there was no editor to protect their readers!

The tendency to keep "bad news" or "bad expectations" at a minimum in the messages was obvious. In 1812 and 1813 and 1814 when Madison had the disagreeable duty of informing Congress of military matters which did not go well for the Americans, he consistently coupled references to adversity with compensating gains. The concluding sections of his 1813 message were typical:

"If the war has increased the interruptions of our commerce, it has at the same time cherished and multiplied our manufactures so as to make us independent of all other countries for the more essential branches for which we ought to be dependent on none. . . .

"If the war has exposed us to increased spoilations on the ocean and to predatory incursions on the land, it has developed the national means of retaliating the former and providing protection against the latter, ...

"In fine, the war, with all its vicissitudes, is illustrating the capacity and the destiny of the United States to be a great, a flourishing, and a powerful nation, worthy of the friendship which it is disposed to cultivate with others, and authorized by its own example to require from all an observance of the laws of justice and reciprocity."[44]

Furthermore, according to Madison, the enemy did not fight fair; a charge which was to be made throughout all war time annual messages. Madison placed much of the blame for American defeats on the British use of the "merciless savages."[45]

In spite of temporary reverses, however, the Presidents were uniform in giving religious thanksgiving for the "advantages which continued to distinguish the lot of the United States from others." The sentiments expressed by Monroe in 1818 were typical: "When we view the great blessings with which our country has been favored, those which we now enjoy, and the means by which we possess of handing them down unimpaired to our latest posterity, our attention is irresistibly drawn to the source from whence they flow. Let us, then, unite in offering our most grateful acknowledgements for these blessings to the Divine Author of All Good."[46]

The Madison annual messages told the story of America's involvement in the titanic struggle being waged between France and England. In 1811 the President recommended that Congress put "the United

States into an armor and attitude demanded by the crisis, and corresponding with the national spirit and expectations." The importance of developments "which occupy the southern portion of our own hemisphere" was noted and the germ of a policy which was to be associated with his Secretary of State James Monroe was projected: "An enlarged philanthropy and an enlightened forecast concur in imposing on the national councils an obligation to take a deep interest in their [Latin-American countries] destinies, to cherish reciprocal sentiments of good will, to regard the progress of events, and not to be unprepared for whatever order of things may be ultimately established."[47]

Unaware of British concessions, Madison called for war in June, 1812 and his subsequent yearly reports told of military and naval action; the customary avoidance of unpleasant particulars was obeyed. He preferred to dwell at greater length on references to the sea battles where Americans won more laurels for bravery. The refusals of the Massachusetts and Connecticut governors to furnish the required number of militia was reported but the extent of the war's unpopularity in New England was played down.

With the Peace of Ghent in 1815, American energy and attention were drawn westward away from trans-Atlantic considerations. Domestic matters monopolized the annual message content almost without exception until the 1890s. Recommendations for a tariff to protect "infant industries" and proposals to promote internal improvements—after constitutional amendment, if necessary—came from Madison on the heels of peace with Great Britain. National sentiments of patriotism and confidence were expressed by Monroe in 1817: "At no period of our political existence had we so much cause to felicitate ourselves at the prosperous and happy condition of our country." The annual messages which followed were all crammed with statistics attesting to the growing strength and material well-being of the country. The westward movement brought Americans more and more in contact with Indians. Gradually, a consistent presidential policy revealed itself: the land would belong to the race that could and would use it. The messages were uniformly optimistic; the "Panic of 1819" was referred to euphemistically as a "pecuniary embarrassment."

While it was true that the average American took little interest in European events, the United States was nevertheless continually involved in diplomatic relations growing out of its position of preeminence in the Western Hemisphere. In 1818 Monroe gave notice that Florida would soon be in the American system and that recognition of the revolutionary Latin-American governments would not be long delayed. The intention of the United States to keep formally aloof from the affairs of the European continent while at the same time exerting a greater influence in the Americas was made official in the annual message of 1823. The extension of Russian claims along the Pacific coast of North America, the threat of the Holy Alliance to restore France and Spain to positions of power in the Western Hemisphere, and the support of Great Britain in opposing this restoration, encouraged Monroe to clarify United States' position.[48] Actually what was later to be known as the "Monroe Doctrine" was not set forth as a specific pronouncement in one part of the annual message. While reporting on negotiations with the Czar concerning Russia's colonizing efforts within the Oregon Territory, Monroe set forth one basic part of the Doctrine: "In the discussions to which this interest has given rise and in the arrangements by which they may terminate the occasion has been judged proper for asserting, as a principle in which the rights and interests of the United States are involved, that the American continents, by the free and independent condition which they have assumed and maintain, are henceforth not to be considered as subjects for future colonization by any European powers.[49]

Having said this, Monroe continued with his detailed survey of foreign affairs and then turned to domestic matters. With the "state of the union" thus fully reported, he added three concluding paragraphs; two of which formed the basis for the remaining parts of the Monroe Doctrine:

"In the wars of the European powers in matters relating to themselves we have never taken any part, nor does it comport with our policy so to do. It is only when our rights are invaded or seriously menaced that we resent injuries or make preparations for our defense. With the movements in this hemisphere we are of necessity more immediately connected, and by causes which must be obvious to all enlightened and impartial observers. The political system of the allied powers is essentially different in this respect from that of America. . . . We owe it, therefore, to candor . . . to declare that we should consider any attempt on their part to extend their system to any portion of this hemisphere as dangerous to our peace and safety. With the existing colonies or dependencies of any European power we have not interfered and shall not interfere. But with the Governments who have declared their independence and maintained it, and whose independence we have, on great consideration and on just principles, acknowledged, we could not view any interposition for the purpose of oppressing them, or controlling in any other manner their destiny, by any European power in any other light than as the manifestation of an unfriendly disposition toward the United States.

" . . . our policy in regard to Europe, which was adopted at an early stage of the wars which have so long agitated that quarter of the globe, nevertheless remain the same, which is, not to interfere in the internal concerns of any of its powers; . . . It is impossible that the allied powers should extend their political system to any portion of either continent without endangering our peace and happiness; nor can anyone believe that our southern brethern, if left to themselves, would adopt it of their own accord."[50]

When John Quincy Adams became President in 1825 the world was enjoying an unusual period of non-violence between the great powers; practically all of his reporting concerned itself with domestic questions. In his first message Adams proposed a program of federally-financed improvements: construction of an adequate system of highways, deepening of harbors and canals, establishment of a national university, building of an astronomical observatory, and the financing of an exploratory expedition to chart the northwest coast of North America. "The spirit of improvement is abroad upon the earth," he said in 1825, and this belief seemed to animate all of his annual message requests. Adams was aware of strong opposition to federal action of the kind he suggested but he reminded Congress that it had many, many powers under the Constitution and he proceeded to enumerate these. He concluded with the admonition that, "to refrain from exercising them for the benefit of the people themselves would be to hide in the earth the talent committed to our charge— would be treachery to the most sacred of trusts."[51] The party of Jefferson had come a long way.

In foreign affairs the annual message of 1825 made the first mention of a "Pan-American Congress," the President reporting that an invitation had been accepted to send American ministers to the meeting in Panama.[52] Domestically the passage of the "Tariff of Abominations" in 1828 brought from Adams a long, partisan defense of the measure. It was the opening shot in a new series of congressional debates which centered on the tariff and subsequently, on the nullification question.

By 1828 the annual message had been shorn of its ceremonial dress and its monarchical flavor. In its place had been substituted a business-like summary, not unlike one which might be submitted by a corporation president to his board of directors. The United States was a growing concern and prospects for the future were bright. The annual message tone in keeping with its function was unemotional, deliberate, and for the most part, uninspiring. In 1827 Adams reiterated the accepted view, mentioned earlier by Monroe and implied by Jefferson and Madison, that: "The purpose of this communication will be to present to your [congressional] view the general aspect of our public affairs at this moment and the measures which have been taken to carry into effect the intentions of the Legislature as signified by the laws then and heretofore enacted."

Chapter Three

PRESIDENTIAL PERSONALITY AND PREDILECTION

The electoral triumph of Andrew Jackson in 1828 was the confirmation of a trend; great changes were underway not only in government but in many other human activities. A new democratic spirit was developing. A tide of social reform and humanitarian idealism had been rising for more than a decade. Jackson was more the product than the creator of these times. "Like Rostand's *Chanteclar*, his crowing did not summon the sun of a new dawn," writes Arthur M. Schlesinger, "but his voice rang out in clarion tones when the morning light was breaking."[1]

Jackson was the first President since Washington whose election was not dependent in any way on Congress—neither for nomination nor election. Further, his victory was practically coincidental with the switch to popular election of presidential electors in most states. Thus he was justified in feeling that he represented the "sovereign will" of the people. Daniel Webster and his Whig colleagues, clearly apprehensive of the future, compared the inauguration of "Old Hickory" with the barbarian invasion of Rome. "I never saw such a mixture," complained Supreme Court Justice Joseph Story. "The reign of King Mob seemed triumphant."

In Andrew Jackson the common people found their first popular leader. His dramatic career was founded on a temperament shaped in large measure by his likes and dislikes. A born leader, he represented the rising West and he was loved for the enemies he made in his fight against the aristocratic East.[2] The farmers of the frontier states had enjoyed universal suffrage almost from the start, and the older seaboard states in order to discourage migration west had reluctantly extended the right to vote to the working class. The urban laborer and the small farmer combined were now able to elect their own champion to the presidency. The Democratic party, successor to the Democratic-Republican one, gradually abandoned the Jeffersonian doctrine of congressional sovereignty and welcomed the vigorous exercise of presidential powers. The Whigs, successors to the Federalists, now saw their political salvation in a legislative supremacy which could impede rapid and drastic changes in the *status quo*.

With Jackson, the growing enfeeblement of the presidency was checked abruptly and decisively. The Jeffersonian transformation of the office was reversed. "Jackson's presidency was, in truth, no mere revival of the office," writes Edward S. Corwin, "it was the remaking of it."[3] In his care the annual message regained its vitality and imprint of a strong personality.

Jackson was the leader of a party organization and he had a program primed for enactment. The constitutional obligation to make recommendations to Congress was no burden to him; he fashioned it into a national platform from which he gave exposition to his policies and appealed for support over the heads of the lawmakers to the public at large. Refusing to be bound by earlier Presidents who had avoided open partisanship in their messages, Jackson devoted a large section of each yearly report to a scolding lecture on a particular issue, usually relating to banking and currency. Congress got more than information; it was given a piece of Jackson's mind. The language in 1834 is typical: "Circumstances make it my duty to call the attention of Congress to the Bank of the United States. Created for the convenience of the Government, that institution has become the scourge of the people."

The following statement in Jackson's 1836 message was characteristic: "It remains to be seen whether the persons who as managers of the old bank undertook to control the Government, retained the public dividends, shut their doors upon a committee of the House of Representatives, and filled the country with panic to accomplish their own sinister objects may now as managers of a new bank continue with impunity to flood the country with a spurious currency, use the seven millions of Government stock for their own profit, and refuse to the United States all information as to the present condition of their own property and the prospect of recovering it into their own possession."[4]

Nor did Jackson confine his outspoken remarks to domestic foes. In 1834 he recommended that reprisals be made upon French property if claims, arising from French depredations on American commerce during the Napoleonic Wars and acknowledged by them, were not provided for at the approaching session of the French chambers. The President argued that if an appropriation was not forthcoming, it could be concluded that France had decided not to honor its obligations and he opposed any further negotiations.

In France, the American minister Edward Livingston was awaiting instructions from the State Department. When none arrived, he depended for guidance on a New York newspaper's reprint of the Jackson annual message. He had promised to bring the President's message to the notice of the French government as soon as possible and when the newspaper came before his diplomatic pouch, Livingston delivered the reprint to Comte de Rigny requesting him at the same time to observe that "it was not an authentic paper, nor was it delivered in pursuance of instructions, nor in my official character." Within three days, however, the French government announced that its minister to the United States was being recalled because of the "provocative" and "irritating" tone of Jackson's annual message. Livingston expressed surprise and regret that a "communication made by one branch of the Government of the United States to another, not addressed to that of His Majesty the King of France, nor even communicated to it" should be "alleged as the motive" for cutting off diplomatic relations.[5] Livingston's explanation was rejected by the Chamber of Deputies but it voted the necessary appropriation on the condition that the money would be paid if President Jackson apologized for his slur against the French nation.[6]

Livingston's insistence that the annual message was really an intra-governmental consultation to which no foreign country could take legitimate exception, was unacceptable to the French. In December, 1835, Jackson in his message to Congress supported his minister's position, asserting in stronger language that "the American people are incapable of submitting to an interference by any government on earth, however powerful, with the free performance of the domestic duties which the Constitution has imposed on their public functionaires." He concluded with the pledge that "The honor of my country shall never be stained by an apology from me for the statement of truth and the performance of duty."[7]

Nevertheless, Jackson did make the conciliatory comment that "The conception that it was my intention to menace or insult the Government of France is as unfounded as the attempt to extort from the fears of that nation what her sense of justice may deny would be vain and ridiculous." Pleased to find in this remark the face-saving device it needed, the French government interpreted the Jackson statement as an "apology."[8] In May of 1836 Jackson announced that the first four of six installments had been paid. His final annual message contained a single sentence reference to France noting that diplomatic relations had been resumed under conditions preserving "mutually beneficial intercourse" and fostering "amicable feelings." Not since Jefferson's abandonment of the in person address had the annual message as a political institution been the cause of such controversy.

The keynote of the Jackson messages was their appeal for public approbation. In 1830 and again in 1834 he departed from traditional practice to include justification of a veto which he had cast against financing internal improvements at federal expense. He capped the lengthy defense of his action by asserting his reliance "upon the intelligence and candor of my fellow-citizens, . . . for a correct appreciation of my motives in interposing as I have done on this and other occasions checks to a course of legislation which, . . . I consider as sanctioning improper and unconstitutional expenditures of public treasure."[9] He considered himself as the only representative of the people as a whole and he felt directly responsible to them.

"I know," Jackson declared in his 1830 message, "of no tribunal to which a public man in this country, in a case of doubt and difficulty, can appeal with greater advantage or more propriety than the judgment of the people; and although I must necessarily in the discharge of my official duties be governed by the dictates of my own judgment, I have no desire to conceal my anxious wish to conform so far as I can to the views of those for whom I act."[10]

With Jackson the messages grew in length, ranging from 6,500 to 14,000 words each. The increase was largely accountable by the detailed attention he gave to recommendations for legislation. His role as a prime mover in the lawmaking process was attested to by Representative Richard Fletcher, a member of the House Ways and Means Committee, who said that the main function of that committee during Jackson's administration was "going through the form of approving the laws which he prepared and handed down to them for acceptance."[11]

The tariff, public debt, office holding, Indians, banking, direct election of the President, currency, internal improvements, nullification, foreign policy—all were discussed fully by Andrew Jackson. In the pages of his annual messages can be discovered the web of political philosophy and administrative policy which has been characterized as the "Jacksonian Revolution."

A succinct passage in his 1829 report set forth his premise on government offices: "The duties of all public officers are, or at least admit of being made, so plain and simple that men of intelligence may readily qualify themselves for their performance; and I can not but believe that more is lost by the long continuance of men in office than is generally to be gained by their experience."[12]

Jackson's opposition to the Bank of the United States was reiterated annually. As early as 1829 he made his position clear: he questioned both the constitutionality and the expediency of the law which created the Bank and charged that "it must be admitted by all that it has failed in the great end of establishing a uniform and sound currency."

The Indian question brought from Jackson a general plan similar to the one laid down by Jefferson and one which became the model for succeeding Presidents until the Civil War. He recommended that "an ample district west of the Mississippi . . . be guaranteed to the Indian tribes so long as they shall occupy it, each tribe having a distinct control over the portion designated for its use."[13] Emigration was to be voluntary but Indians who opted against were to be subject to the laws of the states.

A persistent Jackson recommendation was for a constitutional amendment to correct what he considered abuses in the election of President and Vice President. He called for a change which would insure that no President should be chosen by deals or bargaining in the House of Representatives; but rather "in pursuance of a fair expression of the will of the majority."[14] He also urged the limitation of the President's term to a single one of either four or six years.

Recurrent problems maintained their place in the messages but new ones were also forcing their way to presidential attention. The canal craze and increased mention of rail and ocean mail contracts were reported along with statistics on the sale of public lands, and the proposal that a ship canal be constructed in Central America. A bygone period in American history is nostalgically recalled by Jackson's financial statement of 1835 in which he announced the liquidation of the public debt and expressed the expectation that the Treasury would hold a surplus of about $19,000,000 by the end of the year.[15]

The country's foreign relations were relatively calm during the Jacksonian reign, the controversy with France over spoilation claims constituting the main difficulty. A terse summation of the national posture was provided by the President in his farewell address of 1837: "You have no longer any cause to fear danger from abroad; your strength and power are well known throughout the civilized world, . . . It is from within, among yourselves—from cupidity, from corruption, from disappointed ambition and inordinate thirst for power—that factions will be formed and liberty endangered."[16]

The election of Martin Van Buren in 1836 was considered by the Whigs as the "third term of Andrew Jackson." They recognized correctly that Jackson had picked his successor; seeing this as a precedent, the Whigs predicted the end of the Republic.[17] Time was to prove that their dire forecast was alarmist. The Van Buren annual messages were concerned mainly with banking and finance. The panic of 1837, the worst business and commercial disaster up to that time, did not run its course until 1841. In 1839 the President devoted 7,000 of the message's 12,000 words to an examination of ways and means of dealing with the contemporary economic condition. His position was tersely stated in his final yearly report; referring to a national debt and a national bank he wrote: "Coming into office the declared enemy of both, I have earnestly endeavored to prevent a resort to either."[18]

The relative quiet on the foreign affairs front was broken by disputes with Great Britain arising from conflicting claims over the United States northeastern boundary and charges of neutrality violations during the Canadian Rebellion of 1837. On these matters the Van Buren annual messages reported in great detail. He was, however, no Jackson and this was no secret either to the country or to readers of his "state of the union" reports. The messages were longer but the flashes of presidential lightning were now mere flickers. Congress rested more at ease.

In 1840 the Whigs borrowed a page from the Democratic book of Jacksonian folklore figures and elected William Henry Harrison in a riotous, exuberant campaign in which the wealthy hero of Tippecanoe became the log-cabin, hard-cider "man of the people." The vision of a legislative guardianship over the executive intoxicated many happy Whigs and Daniel Webster patronizingly offered Harrison a prepared inaugural address. The President sensibly declined the offer but let Webster and Henry Clay help with a revision of his own speech. The result was an address which gave full promise that Whig doctrine would be strictly endorsed:

"I can not conceive that by a fair construction any or either of its [constitutional] provisions would be found to constitute the President a part of the legislative power. It can not be claimed from the power to recommend, since, although enjoined as a duty upon him, it is a privilege which he holds in common with every other citizen; and although there may be something more of confidence in the propriety of the measures recommended in the one case than in the other, in the obligations of ultimate decision there can be no difference."[19]

A month after his inaugural, Harrison was dead; he never presented an annual message to Congress. When Vice President John Tyler acceded to the presidency, the Whig victory bonfires were truly in ashes. His subsequent refusal to fall in with Whig policies left Tyler isolated in the White House without support from any party. His conduct of the office, however, did check congressional hopes for a parliamentary monopoly on lawmaking decisions. The annual message continued to arrive in December of each year but, after Jackson, it decreased its appeal to the public at large and perfunctorily served up piles of information for Congress. Tyler's concluding sentence in 1842 typifies the restrained tone of the messages: "I have thus, fellow-citizens, acquitted myself of my duty under the Constitution . . . by inviting your attention to matters of much importance to the country."

The forward march of "manifest destiny" was recorded in the Tyler "state of the union" summations. The settlement reached in the Webster-Ashburton treaty was featured in 1842; his recommendation in 1844 to admit Texas to the union by a joint resolution won support; and his position on Oregon, set forth fully in the messages, gained popular acceptance and historical fame as the memorable slogan of the 1844 election: "Fifty-four, forty or fight!" The continuing debate over banking and currency control, culminating in Tyler's veto of Whig measures to revive earlier banking schemes, was fed by massive presidential statistics and commentary.

James K. Polk was the only strong President between 1837 and 1861. When his use of the veto was challenged by critics who questioned by what authority he interfered with congressional lawmaking, Polk used the annual message of 1848 to deliver a vigorous lecture on what he conceived to be the nature of the federal system. Some cabinet members were doubtful about the propriety of discussing such matters in the yearly report but Polk brushed objections aside. His message explained that "on this last occasion of making to Congress an annual communication 'of the state of the Union' it is not deemed inappropriate to review the principles and considerations which have governed my action." The doctrine of separated powers and an independent executive were affirmed: "The President represents in the executive department the whole people of the United States, as each member of the legislative department represents portions of them." Polk's interpretation of section 2 of article III of the Constitution was precisely set forth:

"When the President recommends measures to Congress, he avows in the most solemn form his opinions, gives his voice in their favor, and pledges himself in advance to approve them if passed by Congress. If he acts without due consideration, or has been influenced by improper or corrupt motives, of if from any other cause Congress, or either House of Congress, shall differ from him in opinion, they exercise their *veto* upon his recommendations and reject them; and there is no appeal from their decision but to the people at the ballot box. These are proper checks upon the Executive, wisely interposed by the Constitution. None will be found to object to them or to wish them removed. It is equally important that the constitutional checks of the Executive upon the legislative branch should be preserved."[20]

At the outset of his administration, Polk dedicated himself to the achievement of a four-point program: reduction of the tariff, re-establishment of the independent treasury, settlement of the Oregon boundary, and acquisition of California. All of these were accomplished before he left office. On these events and the many others which occurred during his single term Polk reported at great length in the most complete annual messages before the 1880s.

His first report was "deemed a proper occasion to reiterate and reaffirm the principle avowed by Mr. Monroe [the Monroe Doctrine] and to state my cordial concurrence in its wisdom and sound policy." However, emphasis was put on "this continent," referring to North America, rather than "these continents," as had Monroe: "The United States, sincerely desirous of preserving relations of good understanding with all nation's, can not in silence permit any European interference on the North American continent, and should any such interference be attempted will be ready to resist it at any and all hazards."[21]

The war with Mexico consumed the greater part of his 1846 and 1847 messages as he traced the causes, the military action, the results, and the ultimate aims of the war. In 1847 Polk set forth the policy of "territorial indemnity" and rejected any other settlement as acknowledging that "our country was wrong and that the war declared by Congress with extraordinary unanimity was unjust. . . . " His view prevailed and his message a year later proudly announced that "we may congratulate ourselves that we are the most favored people on earth." He estimated that with the latest land acquisitions, the

United States was almost as large as the whole of Europe. His description of the fertile lands and confirmation of gold discoveries in California lent impetus to the gold rush.

Polk's messages also reflected the growing strength of the American economy. In 1845 he reported that the commerce of the United States was second to only one power and that "at no distant day we shall probably be inferior to none." In 1846, discussing the settlement of public lands, he claimed that the nation's farmers could "from their immense surplus supply not only the home demand, but the deficiencies of food required by the whole world."[22] But the dark clouds of sectional storms were gathering and Polk was compelled to moderate the optimism of his messages, taking note of anti-slavery agitation—"the only dangerous question which lies in our path." Congress was urged to find middle ground.

Zachary Taylor's first annual message in 1849 contained the re-assurance which the Whigs had labored so long and so hard to obtain: "The Executive has authority to recommend (not to dictate) measures to Congress. Having performed that duty the executive department of the Government can not rightfully control the decision of Congress on any subject of legislation until that decision shall have been officially submitted to the President for approval. The check provided by the Constitution in the clause conferring the qualified veto will never be exercised by me except in the cases contemplated by the fathers of the Republic."[23]

Taylor avoided a full examination of the mounting sectional hostility over the slavery question but did acknowledge the divisive effects which were being caused by the debate over the admission of California as a free state. He paid tribute to the growth of the union and averred that "its dissolution would be the greatest of calamities, and to avert it should be the study of every American." He recommended projects which would result in a physical binding of the nation: an American canal through Nicaragua and a railroad across the Isthmus of Panama, a survey to determine the most suitable route for an intercontinental railway, and a reduction in postage rates.

Vice President Millard Fillmore became President in 1850 after Taylor's death and just in time to lend his support to Clay's compromise which Fillmore described in his annual message of that year as a bundle of laws passed to solve the slavery and territorial questions: "a settlement in principle and substance—a final settle-

ment of the dangerous and exciting subjects which they embraced."
He then gladly turned his attention during his term to less incendiary
matters noting the approaching completion of the Capitol, recommending appropriations for internal improvements, and announcing
Commodore Mathew C. Perry's mission to Japan.

The recapture of the presidency by the Democratic party in 1852
and 1856 with Franklin Pierce and James Buchanan failed to stop
the ebbing away of the presidential exercise of leadership. From
the end of the Mexican War until 1861 the office was at low tide;
the attempt of the national political parties to win support in all
sections resulted in the nomination of second-rate figures with docile
personalities. The importance of the annual message naturally suffered
during the administrations of these irresolute and ineffectual executives. Little attention was given to their opinions; consequently, they
were inclined to withhold them. Everyone seemed to like the arrangement. There were individual, isolated exceptions; in December,
1855, for example, President Pierce initiated the delivery of his
message without having received the customary invitation from Congress to do so. That year the Senate had organized promptly on
December 4th, but the House was beginning a lengthy debate to
choose a Speaker. As long as the election continued, the House remained unorganized, and Pierce withheld his message. By the end
of the month, the House was no nearer to a decision and the President was frustrated by the delay; he wanted the British ministry to
change its Central American policy and he felt it essential that
"American policy be well in the public eye" before Parliamentary
debate began on February 1st.[24]

Pierce tried to persuade House leaders to organize quickly but
fruitless balloting continued. Finally on December 29th the President yielded to the urging of political friends who buttressed their
arguments by reference to British practice and sent his message to
both Houses without invitation. The opening paragraph explained
his action:

"The Constitution of the United States provides that Congress
shall assemble annually on the first Monday of December, and it
has been usual for the President to make no communication of a
public character until advised of their readiness to receive it. I have
deferred to this usage until the close of the first month of the session,
but my convictions of duty will not permit me longer to postpone
the discharge of the obligation enjoined by the Constitution upon

the President 'to give to the Congress information of the state of the Union and recommend to their consideration such measures as he shall judge necessary and expedient'."[25]

When the President's private secretary appeared in the Senate chamber and announced that he had been "directed by the President to deliver a written message and several accompanying documents," the floor was yielded to him and he deposited his parcel with the presiding officer. Business was resumed when suddenly a Senator interrupted the proceedings: "I believe the message which has been received from the President is not of an executive character, but is actually his annual message." Although "sensation and expressions of surprise," were reported by *The Congressional Globe,*[26] the message was read by the clerks immediately.

Not so in the House. By a vote of 126 to 87, the Congressmen refused to have a reading until a Speaker was chosen and formal organization achieved. On the 133rd roll call, coming on February 2, 1856, a Speaker was finally elected but it was not until twelve days later that the House agreed to hear the President's message. Throughout the two months of indecisive balloting, debate ensued over the propriety of the President's having submitted his message without first receiving an invitation to do so from Congress. Support for Pierce's action followed these lines:

"The President knows we are in session and it is his duty to communicate with us."

"This action is unprecedented in American history but it is not unprecedented in parliamentary history. The King of England has communicated with the Parliament and his suggestions debated when no Speaker had been chosen."

"The President has been patient but necessity now may compel him."

"It may be found, after we have heard the message, that instead of the President receiving the censure of members . . . the members, and the country at large, will feel indebted to him for having done it."

"Although the President has passed out of the line of precedent, he is still within the line of constitutional duty. He has his responsibilities under the Constitution just as we do."

"This may be an unprecedented act but never before have we been so long delayed in organizing the Congress to proceed to deal with the public business."[27]

Members who opposed having the annual message read before a Speaker had been agreed upon based their arguments on parliamentary objections. The most typical defense was that "there is not at present a Congress, and that there cannot be a Congress while either branch is unorganized." The prerogatives of the lawmakers were seen to be in danger by a Congressman who declared: "I regard this as an innovation upon the usages of the House and the whole practice of the Government. The Executive department is absorbing very rapidly the powers of the government. For one, I intend now and in the future . . . to strike down every such innovation as long as I have a seat upon this floor."[28] Debate in the House was so tumultuous that the clerk repeatedly complained that it was impossible for him to hear what was being said because of the disorder and uproar.

If the Presidents who followed Jackson were unwilling or unable to match his forceful exercise of executive power, his example of using vituperation in the annual message was not completely lost on them. Lashing out at the abolitionists, Pierce and Buchanan, for instance, accused them of whipping up animosity between residents of slave and free states. Pierce in 1855 exclaimed:

"If the passionate rage of fanaticism and partisan spirit did not force the fact upon our attention, it would be difficult to believe that any considerable portion of the people of this enlightened country could have so surrendered themselves to a fanatical devotion to the supposed interests of the relatively few Africans in the United States as totally to abandon and disregard the intersts of the 25,000,000 Americans; to trample under foot the injunctions of moral and constitutional obligation, and to engage in plans of vindictive hostility against those who are associated with them in the enjoyment of the common heritage of our national institutions."[29]

The general pattern of the messages remained unchanged. There was the religious thanksgiving at the outset, then a superficial review of foreign affairs followed by a detailed summation of departmental reports with their accumulation of statistics, and finally a paragraph expressing confidence in the future of the nation. The greater part of the bulk consisted of a factual compendium with a complete Treasury report a permanent feature. Jackson in 1836 had even attached a chart to illustrate his recommended distribution of a $30,000,000 federal surplus but this graphic innovation was not copied by any of the Presidents until the 1870s. The habit of devoting a large section of the message to a particular subject persisted. Where Jackson, Van Buren and Tyler made comprehensive references to banking and finance, the later Presidents of the pre-Civil War period expounded at great length on the issues of territorial expansion, the Mexican War, the nature of the union, and slavery.

The time-honored salutation "Fellow-Citizens of the Senate and House of Representatives" retained its popularity. Nor did the style of religious thanksgiving change though it was becoming more common to restrict such pronouncements to the opening, or in a few messages, the closing paragraphs. Jackson's greeting in 1830 was typical: "The pleasure I have in congratulating you upon your return to your constitutional duties is much heightened by the satisfaction which the condition of our beloved country at this period justly inspires. The beneficent Author of All Good has granted to us during the present year health, peace, and plenty, and numerous causes for joy in the wonderful success which attends the progress of our free institutions."[30]

Even President Buchanan, in the troubled times of December, 1859 paid "deep and heartfelt gratitude . . . to that Almighty Power which has bestowed upon us such varied and numerous blessings" and notwithstanding the demerits of the past year, he assured his readers that "we have much reason to believe from the past events in our history that we have enjoyed the special protection of Divine Providence ever since our origin as a nation."

The disposition to view the country's development with pride and satisfaction was shared by all the Presidents. Jackson, referring to the nearly half century of previous messages, summed up the feeling of official contentment in 1831: "Generally these communications have been of the most gratifying nature, testifying an advance in all the improvements of social and all the securities of political life." A belief in the superiority of the American people and the American system never wavered. The Presidents minimized contemporary problems and maximized the expectation of things to come. Only in retrospect were difficulties likely to be admitted. For example, Buchanan gave the reassuring report in 1857 that "Our relations with foreign countries are upon the whole in a satisfactory condition." Yet three years later he confided to Congress that "When I entered upon the duties of the presidential office, the aspect neither of our foreign nor domestic affairs was at all satisfactory." His 1859 report revealed explicitly the reluctance to discuss distasteful current events: "Whilst it is the duty of the President 'from time to time to give to Congress information of the state of the Union,' I shall not refer in detail to the recent sad and bloody occurrences at Harpers Ferry."

Compared to the pre-Jacksonian messages, however, there was a

marked improvement toward more realistic appraisals of the national
situation. A strong President had to acknowledge shortcomings in
the conditions of the country and take public notice of his critics or
lose the occasion to defend his executive action. Polk apparently
was motivated by such considerations when he complained in his
1846 message of "misapprehensions which have to some extent prevailed as to its [Mexican War] origin and true character." He went
on to spell out in 11,000 words "of the injuries we had sustained, of
the causes which led to the war, and of its progress since its commencement." The slavery issue also influenced the necessity for some
realistic reporting. From 1790 onward the Presidents had exhibited
a uniform inability to pronounce the word or refer to the institution
of slavery. Jackson made the first overt reference in 1836 when he
recommended a law to prohibit the circulation of anti-slavery literature through federal mails. By the 1850s, however, the "gentleman's
agreement" for a moratorium on the public treatment of the slavery
question was beyond extension, and the annual messages contained
frank warnings of disaster which would result if sectional agitation
was not moderated.

But the slavery question remained and would not be quieted. After
1850 the abolitionists were consistently singled out for castigation in
the annual messages as one of the groups responsible for fomenting
radical doctrines and working against the national interest. In his
inaugural address Buchanan expressed the hope that sectional strife
might be laid to rest as a result of the approaching decision of the
Supreme Court in the Dred Scott case. But the Court's verdict
served to inflame the issue and the President struggled through four
years supplying ineffective leadership. His final message, delivered
on December 3, 1860 with Lincoln already elected and South Carolina
preparing to quit the union, reflected Buchanan's inability to take a
strong course:

"How easy would it be for the American people to settle the slavery
question forever and to restore peace and harmony to this distracted
country! They, and they alone, can do it. All that is necessary to
accomplish the object, and all for which the slave States have ever
contended, is to be let alone and permitted to manage their domestic
institutions in their own way. As sovereign States, they and they
alone, are responsible before God and the world for the slavery
existing among them. For this the people of the North are not more
responsible and have no more right to interfere than with similar
institutions in Russia or in Brazil."[31]

The slavery issue, important as it was, did not monopolize presidential attention. The country was not standing still while awaiting the outcome of the momentous dispute. Pierce's messages supplied the following "signs of the times" observations: that successive census returns revealed "a law of steady, progressive development which may be stated in general terms as a duplication of population every quarter century;" that although United States foreign commerce was about equal to that of England the latter had a navy at least ten times as large; that there had been "marine disasters of the most tragic nature, involving great loss of human life"; and that the franking privilege ought to be abolished. Brigham Young drew Buchanan's wrath. He accused him of being the despotic ruler of the Mormons in Utah and of being the leader of the first rebllion that ever existed in United States territory. Calling for decisive military action against Young and his followers, the President explained his stand:

"With the religious opinions of the Mormons, as long as they remained mere opinions, however deplorable in themselves and revolting to the moral and religious sentiments of all Christiandom, I had no right to interfere. Actions alone, when in violation of the Constitution and laws of the United States, become the legitimate subjects for the jurisdiction of the civil magistrate. My instructions to Governor Cummings have therefore been framed in strict accordance with these principles."[32]

The Indian "problem" persisted; the land "guaranteed" to the tribes was continually rolled back. Buchanan proved to be a shortsighted seer when he "indulged in the agreeable anticipation" that at no very distant day the "tribes of Cherokees, Choctaws, Chickasaws, and Creeks settled in the Territory set apart for them west of Arkansas . . . will be incorporated into the Union as one of the soverign states." The concluding paragraph of his final message sounds strangely contemporaneous one hundred years after he wrote it in 1860. Referring to the almost total failure of crops in parts of Kansas, Buchanan reported the destitution to be so general that private contributions could not enable the farmers to buy the necessities of life. Under these circumstances, he urged congressional consideration and stated that "If any constitutional measure for their relief can be devised, I would recommend its adoption."

Domestic questions aside, Cuba was the focus of attention for all the Presidents in the 1850s. Southern annexationists were actively supporting island revolutionists. A large section of Fillmore's 1851 message reported in detail on the ill-fated Lopez filibustering expedi-

tion. The President's opposition to any annexation was defended in
1852: "It would bring into the Confederacy a population of a different
national stock, speaking a different language and not likely to har-
monize with the other members." Pierce and Buchanan, however,
were of a different mind; they counseled the acquisition of Cuba.
Pierce gave his approval to formulation of the Ostend Manifesto
which threatened Spain with force if she did not sell the island, and
Buchanan's recommendation in 1858 that Cuba be purchased was
repeated in his messages of 1859 and 1860.

Relations with Great Britain had always commanded the largest
part of the section on foreign affairs. Buchanan correctly observed
in 1858 that "It has been the misfortune of both countries, almost
ever since the period of the Revolution, to have been annoyed by a
succession of irritating and dangerous questions, threatening their
friendly relations." His conclusion did not apply exclusively to that
year: "In fact, no two countries ever existed on the face of the
earth which could do each other so much good or so much harm."
Buchanan's 1860 hope regarding the treaty signed with Japan did
not prove so prophetic, that "in the language of the treaty itself . . .
'there shall henceforth be perpetual peace and friendship between
the United States of America and His Majesty the Tycoon of Japan
and his succcssors.'" Domestic affairs, however, held presidential
notice in the 1850s; for the first time reporting on foreign affairs
was left almost consistently to the final parts of the annual messages.

From 1829 to 1861 with the exception of the Jackson and Polk
administrations, the annual message was employed less as an instrument of executive leadership and more as a factual summary of presidential law enforcement. The compulsion to present "all the facts"
led to a steady increase in the message verbiage. Jackson used an
average of 10,000 words for each message; none of his successors up
to the Civil War used less than 7,000, and Polk consistently needed
more than 14,000 words each time he gave Congress a "state of the
union" report. Style suffered. Literary flourishes all but disappeared
and where they remained the exceptions were incongruous as when,
for example, in the midst of mundane reporting Polk expressed the
confidence that Texas "will never have cause to regret that she has
united her 'lone star' to our glorious constellation." Elegance of
language seemed a luxury to Presidents weighed down under the
burdens of their office; the document was heavy and grim. Humor

was conspicuously absent; dignity was the implied tone although it was abandoned for a moment in isolated fits of temper.

Of side light interest is Fillmore's annual message of 1850 in which he combined an inaugural address with an annual message. This occurred when he became President in July after Taylor's death in office and did not issue an inaugural statement, as had Tyler in similar circumstances in 1841, but waited until December when he used the first 1,300 words of his annual message for this purpose and devoted the next 6,000 words to his "state of the union" review. It remains the only "two-in-one bargain" to date.

Likewise, well out of the usual run of message commentary which studiously avoided reference to presidential campaigns was Buchanan's 1860 analysis of Lincoln's victory: " . . . the election of any one of our fellow-citizens to the office of President does not of itself afford just cause for dissolving the Union. This is more especially true if his election has been affected by a mere plurality, and not a majority of the people, and has resulted from transient and temporary causes, which may properly never again occur."

Still, no matter how inefficacious and impotent had been the recent presidential incumbents, the office was held in some esteem. The best evidence was South Carolina's decision to trigger the secessionist movement as a result of Lincoln's election. Assurances that the President possessed no absolute powers and that Congress and the Supreme Court were safely in Democratic hands were not successfully dissuasive. So profoundly had Jackson and Polk effected the presidency that not even a succession of self-denying chief executives had erased the memory of what a strong President could do.

Chapter Four

STATE OF THE UNION AT THE CROSSROADS

When Abraham Lincoln became President in March, 1861, seven Southern states had already passed ordinances of secession. His winning majority in the electoral college had been achieved by support of only 40% of the popular vote in a four-cornered race. He was the chief executive of a divided country and the leader of a mongrel political party which included anti-Nebraska Democrats, Free-Soilers, anti-slavery Whigs, and Know-Nothings as well as Republicans. Little was known about his attitude toward the presidency. A large element of the new Republican Party cherished the Whig tradition of legislative supremacy; they felt confident that Lincoln who had been a harsh critic of Polk's war policy would let Congress lead. When a Whig member of Congress years before Lincoln had written: "Were I President, I should desire the legislation of the country to rest with Congress, uninfluenced in its origin or progress, and undisturbed by the veto unless in very special and clear cases."[1]

With the firing on Fort Sumter, however, Lincoln assumed the position that the President must use every means consistent with saving the union. He accepted in principle the separation of powers doctrine but under the pressure of civil war he "pushed the boundaries of executive power . . . over into the legislative sphere" more than any other President before or since.[2] Presidential government in contrast to parliamentary was established.[3]

Congress tried to check-mate Lincoln through the creation of a Joint Committee on the Conduct of the War to share with him control of military planning. By 1862 the hybrid Republican party showed signs of splitting into two wings: the Conservatives favored Lincoln's conciliatory policy toward the South; the Radicals, mainly abolitionists, attacked his program and use of executive power. The struggle between President and Congress became intense over control of Southern reconstruction. Lincoln maintained that the pardoning power of the chief executive made him the appropriate reconstructor. The Radicals refused to co-operate. When their plan drew a presidential veto, they issued the Wade-Davis Manifesto which reaffirmed the traditional Whig doctrine of legislative supre-

44

macy: " . . . the *authority of Congress* is *paramount* and must be respected; . . . and if he [Lincoln] wishes our support he must confine himself to his executive duties—*to obey and execute* not to make the laws—to suppress by arms armed rebellion, and leave political reorganization to Congress." [4]

Radical support of Lincoln in 1864 was markedly unenthusiastic. He was re-elected by a large electoral majority but with a plurality of only 400,000 votes of the four million cast in union territory. Andrew Johnson, a War Democrat from a seceded state, was picked as Lincoln's running-mate to emphasize the administration's determination to restore the nation.

Faced with implacable opposition in Congress to his policies and his conduct of the presidential office, Lincoln needed public support. The wide circulation and the importance attached to the annual message made it perfectly suited to his needs. During his administration it became the medium for his most important policy pronouncements. A constitutional "duty," once again as with Jackson, became a welcome opportunity for a strong willed President to address the nation. A message presumably addressed to Congress was used instead as a loudspeaker by which the President secured an audience rating which could not be matched by any congressional document.

In his first annual message Lincoln departed from the time honored practice of surveying foreign affairs. "It is not my purpose to review our discussions with foreign states", he explained, "because whatever might be their wishes or dispositions, the integrity of our country and the stability of our Government mainly depend not on them, but on the loyalty, virtue, patriotism, and intelligence of the American people. The correspondence itself, with the usual reservations, is herewith submitted." [5]

He sacrificed detailed factual reporting in favor of discussing administration proposals. More emphasis was placed on readability and impact. None of Lincoln's "state of the union" messages exceeded 8,000 words, constituting a temporary reversal of a more voluble trend. Statistical bulk was kept to a minimum by greater dependence on the transmission of cabinet reports to Congress. "These reports," Lincoln reasoned in 1862, "though lengthy are scarcely more than brief abstracts of the very numerous and extensive transactions and operations conducted through those [War and Navy] Departments. Nor could I give a summary of them here on any principle which would admit of its being much shorter than the reports themselves. I therefore content myself with laying the reports before you and asking your attention to them."⁶

It was in his annual message of 1862 that Lincoln set forth his favorite scheme for solving the slavery question and restoring the union without further bloodshed. He embodied in the communication to Congress the draft of a constitutional amendment which provided for compensated emancipation. The magnitude of this intrusion into the lawmaking process was unprecedented.

Lincoln pleaded with the legislators to act favorably on his proposal. Arguing that "Without slavery the rebellion could never have existed; without slavery it could not continue," he "begged indulgence" to discuss his proposition at length. He knew that the proposed amendment would not be popular in Congress but he challenged the legislators to suggest a better course of action if they could:

"Is it doubted, then, that the plan which I propose, if adopted would shorten the war, and thus lessen its expenditure of money and blood? Is it doubted that it would restore the national authority and national prosperity and perpetuate both indefinitely? Is it doubted that we here—Congress and Executive—can secure its adoption? Will not the good people respond to a united and earnest appeal from us? Can we, can they, by any other means so certainly or so speedily assure these vital objects? . . . The dogmas of the quiet past are inadequate to the stormy present. The occasion is piled high with difficulty, and we must rise with the occasion. As our case is new, so we must think anew and act anew. We must disenthrall ourselves, and then we shall save our country."⁷

The appeal was unsuccessful, principal objection coming from legislative representatives of the border states. On January 1, 1863, Lincoln issued the Emancipation Proclamation which declared free all slaves in areas still in rebellion against the United States. By annual message time in December, union forces had severed the Confederacy and turned back Lee at Gettysburg, thrusting the emotion laden issue of reconstruction to the fore. The responsibility of restoring the South was assumed by Lincoln as an executive function exercised by virtue of the pardoning power of the President. It was his contention that no state had ever left the union; he most often referred to the southern states as the "so-called seceded states," and to the war as an "insurrection" but he also used the term "civil war" on a few occasions. Along with his "state of the union" report, he sent to Congress in 1863 a Proclamation of Amnesty and Reconstruction, thus capitalizing on the attention which was naturally drawn to his annual message. He discussed the proclamation in the communication, once again using the "duty to report" as a means of explaining administration policy to the national audience.

Likewise the next year Lincoln demonstrated his penchant for employing the yearly message as an important presidential mouthpiece. After sweeping briskly over routine matters, he attempted to reach behind the Confederate lines and drive a wedge between its leader, Jefferson Davis, and the southern citizenry. The President disclaimed the possibility of negotions between the "insurgent leader" and the union because "he will not voluntarily reaccept the Union and we will not yield it." But Lincoln argued: "What is true . . . of him who heads the insurgent cause is not necessarily true of those who follow. Although he can not reaccept the Union, they can. Some of them, we know, already desire peace and reunion. The number of such may increase. They can at any moment have peace simply by laying down their arms and submitting to the national authority under the Constitution."[8]

Lincoln reiterated his terms for ending the hostilities: "In stating a single condition of peace I mean simply to say that the war will cease on the part of the Government whenever it shall have ceased on the part of those who began it."

Under Lincoln's pen, the annual message reached one of its highest peaks of prestige and consequence. Factual reporting continued but on a smaller and less detailed scale. As the presidency itself became more forceful, the annual report became correspondingly more significant; and conversely, Lincoln's dramatic use of the message made a distinct contribution to the up-grading of the office. George Fort Milton thinks that Lincoln's handling of public opinion surpassed all other functions which he was called upon to perform.[9]

The great theme of the Lincoln messages was war and reconstruction. It ran like a thread through his four yearly reports in which he laid out his policies for winning the war, solving the slavery dilemma, and restoring the union to its pre-war political entity. In 1861 he told Congress of his determination that the insurrection should not "degenerate into a violent and remorseless revolutionary struggle" and that the integrity of the union should be the "primary object of the contest on our part." He suggested a plan whereby freed slaves might be encouraged to colonize "at some place or places in a climate congenial to them" and added that free Negroes, if they so desired, might be included in such colonization.

Lincoln reiterated the following year his strong support of Negro settlement overseas when pressing for adoption of his constitutional amendment for compensated emancipation. It was his opinion that the North bore equal responsibility for the introduction of slavery to America, had shared equally in the profits of slave labor and that the South should be paid for loss of its property. "It may not be quite safe," he said, "to say [of slavery] that the South has been more responsible than the North for its continuance."[10] He interpreted his re-election in 1864 as a mandate to free all the slaves including those in states which had not been in rebellion and he urged Congress to achieve this total Negro liberation by amending the Constitution. Lincoln called for the abandonment of armed resistance to the national authority but warned that this action would not erase the steps he had taken to abolish slavery:

"I repeat the declaration made a year ago that 'while I remain in my present position I shall not attempt to retract or modify the emancipation proclamation, nor shall I return to slavery any person who is free by the terms of that proclamation or by any of the acts of Congress.' If the people should, by whatever mode or means, make it an Executive duty to reenslave such persons, another, and not I, must be their instrument to perform it."[11]

Other subjects of importance were duly noted. In 1862 Lincoln pointed out that public lands had practically ceased to be a source of revenue and that the homestead laws taking effect would be such an inducement to settlers that sales for cash could not be expected to meet the expenses of the General Land office and the cost of surveying and bringing the land into market. Indians in the same year were reported to have killed at least eight hundred people and a year later the President wrote "Indian disturbances in New Mexico have not been entirely suppressed." He noted also the great shortage of labor and recommended that Congress give assistance to the "tens of thousands . . . thronging our foreign consulates and offering to emigrate to the United States." In 1864 he called for the admission of more immigrants: "one of the principal replenishing streams which are appointed by Providence to repair the ravages of internal war." Progress was reported in the construction of a transcontinental railroad and telegraph system, and Lincoln gave his support to projects envisioning trans-Atlantic and trans-Pacific telegraph cable connections. "Business as usual" was reported even as the fate of the national enterprise itself was in doubt.

The South was told in 1864 that the union could maintain "the contest indefinitely" if need be because the North's population was increasing; the "important fact remains demonstrated that we have *more* men *now* than we had when the war *began*." This increase in number was proven, said Lincoln, by the election returns of 1864. "Compared with the surviving, the fallen have been so few" or else "so many voters could not have been found." Honest Abe's census yardstick might be challenged by cynics!

The Radicals welcomed Lincoln's assassination as a deliverance of the executive office into their hands. They felt confident that Andrew Johnson would defer to the dictates of Congress. In this they were mistaken. Johnson's decision to carry Lincoln's reconstruction plan forward guaranteed that the rivalry between the executive and legislative branches would continue. The Radicals were determined to assert their mastery over the presidency as well as over the South. Johnson alone stood in their way and this awareness led him to enter into a deception when the time came for his first annual message to Congress in December, 1865. In his biography of George Bancroft, Russell Nye tells what happened:

"The Radicals were already organizing, and Johnson's greatest hope lay in a direct appeal to the people for support in the approaching combat with the conspirators. Johnson knew what he wanted to say in his message. The difficulty was that the President's political oratory, a product of the Tennessee hustings, was hardly the vehicle designed to make its presentation impressive. George Bancroft could simply say it better, and as early as October the two men entered into an agreement, Bancroft to write the message, keeping his authorship a secret, and Johnson to give it as his own."[12]

This "state of the union" report was assumed at the time to have been written by the President and received almost unanimous acclaim as a model of message form. It was replete with extravagant praise of the Constitution, its framers, and the American political system. Johnson's hope to acquire the Lincoln mantle of leadership by impressing Congress with this overwhelmingly masterful communication failed. The congressional elections of 1866 gave the Radicals enough votes to overcome Johnson vetoes; the independence of the executive was erased and a quasi-parliamentary system was in effect.[13]

The rebuke by Congress worked a tremendous transformation in the language of the Johnson messages. In 1867, fighting for his political life, he took firm hold of his best weapon to lash out at his antagonists. He ripped the veneer of diplomatic gloss from the mes-

sage and under the guise of reporting to Congress denounced that
body publicly. As the jumping off point, he declared that it was a
"source of profound regret" that he was unable to announce "any
definitive adjustment, satisfactory to the American people" concerning
reconstruction. "On the contrary," he said, "candor compels me to
declare that at this time there is no Union as our fathers understood
the term."

Johnson charged that acts of Congress were not only objectionable
for their assumption of ungranted power but that many of their
provisions were in direct conflict with prohibitions of the Constitution.
Pressing the fight Johnson denounced the congressional plan of reconstruction as the "most unreasonable that could be invented." He
disclaimed any desire to be lenient to those who perpetrated the
rebellion but insisted that the reconstructed states were entitled to
a republican form of government as guaranteed by the Constitution.
Johnson appealed to his national audience for support, condemning
the military occupation of the South:

"It binds them hand and foot in absolute slavery, and subjects
them to a strange and hostile power, more unlimited and more
likely to be abused than any other now known among civilized men.
It tramples down all those rights in which the essence of liberty
consists, . . . It denies *habeas corpus* and the trial by jury. Personal
freedom, property, and life, if assailed by the passion, the prejudice,
or the rapacity of the ruler, have no security whatever. It has the
effect of a bill of attainder or bill of pains and penalties, not upon
a few individuals, but upon the whole masses, including the millions
who inhabit the subject States, and even their unborn children."[14]

Johnson's most vitriolic attacks were directed at the laws giving
suffrage to the Negro in the South. In his bristling onslaught
he completely abandoned the traditional dignity of the annual
message to berate Congress and its program. Charging that "Negro
domination would be worse than military despotism," he warned that
it was "worse than madness" to expect that Negroes would be able
to help govern the South at that time. He implored that "if anything
can be proved by known facts, if all reasoning upon evidence is not
abandoned, it must be acknowledged that in the progress of nations
negroes have shown less capacity for government than any other
race of people. No independent government of any form has ever
been successful in their hands. On the contrary, wherever they
have been left to their own devices they have shown a constant
tendency to relapse into barbarism."[15]

Johnson continued to battle Congress with gloves off until the expiration of his term. His reports on the "state of the union" had not neglected the routine matters which all Presidents alluded to, but the emphasis had been more on the state of the President's differences with Congress. No attempt was made to conceal his utter contempt for the lawmakers. The tumultuous reconstruction era overshadowed Johnson's view of the union from 1865 to 1869. Foreign affairs reporting, as with Lincoln, got short shrift usually showing up at the tail end of the message. A noteworthy item was the reference in 1866 to the agreement of France to withdraw its troops from Mexico. Signs of renewed interest in territorial expansion—harbingers of colonial building proclivities—were the President's reminder to Congress that the appropriation to Russia for the cession Alaska was due, his observation that the West Indies may be expected "ultimately to be absorbed by the continental States, including our own;" and his conviction that the people of the Hawaiian Islands "shall of themselves, at no distant day, voluntarily apply for admission into the Union."

The war's residue was represented by the President's comment about the "unprecedented extent" of the swelled pension rolls, and his 1866 summation from the war department report: "More than 6,000 maimed soldiers have received artificial limbs or other surgical apparatus, and 41 national cemeteries, containing the remains of 104,526 Union soldiers, have already been created." The westward movement underway in full blast was symbolized by the President's references to the "throngs of immigrants that crowd our shores," the completion of the transcontinental railway, and the reversal of the traditional American public land policy which now placed settlement before revenue.[16]

The smoldering banking and currency questions, stifled in the 1850s by the approaching war and all but smothered by it, burst forth again to remain one of the perennial subjects talked about by the Presidents. Johnson in 1865 restated the traditional presidential view: "We should look at the national debt just as it is—not as a national blessing, but as a heavy burden on the industry of the country, to be discharged without unnecessary delay." He didn't get his way. Before leaving office he took a final swipe at Congress. Except for the sprinkling of vituperation, his thesis would sound natural coming from a present-day foe of big budgets and deficit financing:

We now pride ourselves upon having given freedom to 4,000,000

of the colored race; it will then be our shame that 40,000,000 of
people, by their own toleration of usurpation and profligacy, have
suffered themselves to become enslaved, and merely exchanged slave
owners for new taskmaskers in the shape of bondholders and taxgatherers. Besides, permanent debts pertain to monarchical governments, and, tending to monopolies, perpetuities, and class legislation,
are totally irreconcilable with free institutions."[17]

Johnson also joined the ranks of chief executives opposed to the
electoral college; he recommended direct election of the President
and Vice President with single terms for both, specific designation
of the person who should become President in the event of the
inability of both President and Vice President to serve; and direct
election of United States Senators.[18]

Ulysses S. Grant was a fitting antidote to Andrew Johnson. Those
who believed that they had in him a new tribune of the people—
a second coming of Andrew Jackson—were quickly disillusioned.
Grant's concept of the presidency cheered the Whig faction of the
Republican party which had searched so diligently and unsuccessfully for his prototype. His final annual message, looking back
over his eight years in office, gave a clue to the spirit with which he
had approached his duty in 1869: "It [reconstruction] was the work
of the legislative branch. . . . My province was wholly in approving
their acts, which I did most heartily." Perfunctory annual messages
began to flow once again from the Grant occupied White House to
the Capitol. In the hands of a chief executive who had no quarrel
with Congress and no wish to re-heat the cooling cauldrons of controversy, the yearly document abruptly resumed its pre-Civil War
deference. The rancor of Johnson's attacks disappeared as his successor proceeded to submit moderate, conciliatory, bland messages.
By the end of his second term the Senate had reached its pinnacle of
power and Congress was giving the orders.

Under Grant the dutiful summary of foreign and domestic affairs—
mainly the summation of departmental reports—again became the
dominant part of the annual message. Occasionally, he used headings to facilitate finding information more quickly, and sometimes
the status of federal finances was presented in chart form. His attitude toward the function of the annual message is indicated by this
characteristic statement in 1871: "I have thus hastily summed up
the operations of the Government during the last year, and made such
suggestions as occur to me to be proper for your consideration. I

submit them with a confidence that your combined action will be wise, statesmanlike, and in the best interests of the whole country."[19]

Grant's annual messages were concerned chiefly with domestic matters: reconstruction, the tariff, resumption of species payments, and civil service reform. His feeling about treatment of the Indians was expressed pithily: "From the foundation of the Government to the present the management of the original inhabitants of this continent . . . has been a subject of embarrassment and expense, and has been attended with continuous robberies, murders, and wars."[20] His opinion that neither legislation nor the conduct of the whites had been "blameless for these hostilities" was refreshingly objective. In 1869 he announced his intention of enlisting the aid of the Society of Friends to help manage the Indians but four years later a less conciliatory Grant reported that it had been his policy "to collect the Indians as rapidly as possible on reservations, and as far as practicable within what is known as the Indian Territory, and to teach them the arts of civilization and self-support. Where found off these reservations, and endangering the peace and safety of the whites, they have been punished, and will continue to be for like offenses."[21]

Troublesome white groups also caused him concern; the Klu Klux Klan and the Mormons in particular drew his fire.[22] The attention of Congress was invited to the evil of the "importation of Chinese women, but few of whom are brought to our shores to pursue honorable or useful occupations." Signs of the times were evidenced by Grant's recommendations that the income tax be renewed (at a reduced rate of three per cent); that the free delivery of mail be extended to all cities with a population of not less than 10,000; that perhaps the Supreme Court should be increased to eleven members; and that American steamships should receive mail contract subsidies to help build up the merchant marine.

Grant repeated other specific recommendations throughout his administration usually without effect: direct election of the President and Vice President; the "item veto" power for the President; limitation on Congress at extra sessions to the consideration of only those issues presented by the President; a constitutional duty that each state furnish equal elementary school education for all children "irrespective of sex, color, birthplace, or religion"; and the taxation of all church and corporation property on an equal basis, "excepting only the last resting place of the dead and possibly, with proper restrictions, church edifices."

In foreign affairs, Grant noted and discussed the outbreak of revolution in Cuba, the activities of the Fenians along the Canadian border, and the settlement of differences with Great Britain by arbitration. He announced in 1871 that "for the first time in the history of the United States as a nation" there was no boundary dispute with the English. His favorite project, the annexation of Santo Domingo, was urged in practically every message.[23]

The election of Rutherford B. Hayes coming as it did as part of the "Crime of '76" was reassuring to congressional leaders. Victors over the defiant Johnson and manipulators of the popular idol Grant, they confidently expected little interference from the new White House resident. But President Hayes, pledged in advance to a single term, conducted the executive office in marked contrast to the timid Grant. Subservience to the Radicals was no longer the watchword; the long decline in dignity and prestige of the presidency was halted. His rebuff of congressional hegemony is a milestone not because of any great increase of presidential power but more for the successful defense against further encroachment.

Hayes pursued a limited program: restoration of harmony between North and South, institution of civil service reform, and maintenance of the gold standard as long as necessary to revive business. But it was a program of his own and he used the annual message as an instrument to persuade and pressure Congress. Resorting to the compendium technique, popular in the 1840s, he singled out only one or two important issues for detailed examination and argumentation. However, his approach was cautious and apologetic; legislative initiative had swung completely to Congress.

Hayes' reference to the silver coinage debate, in his 1877 message, is indicative of his wariness: "Without intruding upon this province of legislation in the least, I have yet thought the subject of such critical importance, . . . as to present an occasion for the exercise of the duty imposed by the Constitution on the President of recommending to the consideration of Congress 'such measures as he shall judge necessary and expedient.' "[24]

In 1877 Hayes reported the withdrawl of federal troops from the South. This reference marked the end of lengthy presidential commentary on reconstruction and the beginning of increased attention to western movement, currency and banking legislation, and civil service reform. Foreign affairs attracted little interest; the low point was reached in 1878 when Hayes devoted almost as much space to District of Columbia business as he did to his report on the rest of

the world. Many of the problems which had vexed Grant contin
through the Hayes administration. Utah remained a trouble sp
specie payments were defended, and Indians remained on the war-
path. The desirability of federal aid to the states "for the education
of the whole people in those branches of study which are taught
in the common schools," said the President in 1877, "is no longer a
question." In fact, he continued, "intelligent judgment of the
country" goes further in favoring federal aid for technical and
higher education. Hayes alluded to the sentiments expressed by
Washington in 1790 that education was especially important for the
success of a free government where the people are the source of
power; he deplored the fact that "one-seventh of the entire voting
population of our country were unable to read and write."

The administrations of James A. Garfield and Chester A. Arthur
were carried on under the umbrella of congressional authority.
The cyclical movement of presidential power was again demonstrated
when from 1865 to 1885, as from 1809 to 1829 and from 1837 to 1861,
Congress was the dominant branch of the federal government. With
the exception of Hayes, each of the Presidents between Lincoln and
Cleveland were fearful of the Radical oligarchy; the period marked
the heaviest political attacks ever made on either the person, the
office or the power of the President.[25]

Garfield died in office before annual message time. His successor,
Arthur, uttered probably the most feeble of all presidential "recommendations." Referring to the congressional consideration of
a tax reduction in 1881 he commented: "In fulfillment of what I deem
my constitutional duty, but with little hope that I can make valuable
contribution to this vexed question, I shall proceed to intimate
briefly my own views in relation to it."[26]

It was pusilanimity at its most abject. Small wonder that James
Bryce was then recording the observation that: "The expression of
his [the President's] wishes conveyed in a message has not necessarily
any more effect on Congress than an article in a prominent party
newspaper . . . and in fact the suggestions which he makes year
after year, are usually neglected, even when his party has a majority
in both Houses, or when the subject lies outside party lines."[27]

The two outstanding contributions of the Arthur administration
were in civil service reform and in the increase of United States naval
strength. His recommendation for "decisive action" to correct the
evils of the patronage system pre-dated the passage of the Pendleton

Act by less than two months, and the construction of modern steel warships followed Arthur's insistence in his 1880 annual message on a "thorough rehabilitation" of the navy. Two new topics, conservation and railroad legislation, came in for increased mention. In 1883 the President asked Congress as far as constitutionally possible to "protect the people at large in their interstate traffic against acts of injustice which the State governments are powerless to prevent."

Arthur's "state of the union" was good: Sitting Bull was in jail and the Secretary of War reported that there had been just one disturbance among the Indians; the free delivery mail system had been extended to 159 cities; and the "colossal statue of Liberty Enlightening the World, the generous gift of the people of France [was] expected to reach New York in May next [1885]." Like his immediate predecessors, Arthur called for the eradication of pologamy and punishment of the Mormons, but for the most part he appeared to be content. The placidness extended to foreign affairs where Arthur assured Congress that "The feelings of good will between our country and that of Great Britain was never more marked than at present."

Secretary of State James G. Blaine's call for a Latin-American peace conference and Arthur's subsequent postponement of it was duly noted in 1882 and the opening for commerce of "the rich and populous valley of the Kongo . . . by a society called the International African Association, of which the King of the Belgians is the president" was mentioned in 1883. Conclusion of a treaty with Nicaragua "which authorizes the construction by the United States of a canal, railway, and telegraph line across the Nicaraguan territory" was reported with evident gratification.

Arthur's repeated recommendation that Congress legislate on the question of what to do when the President was incapacitated was not heeded. His experience of standing by for two months as President Garfield lingered before succumbing to his fatal wounding had made an understandable impression on the waiting then Vice President. The concluding paragraph of his final annual message renewed the following recommendations: "The preservation of forests on the public domain, the granting of government aid for popular education ,the amendment of the federal Constitution so as to make effective the disapproval by the President of particular items in appropriation bills, . . . and the determining of vexed questions respecting presidential inability."

1884 signaled the end of the post-war Republican monopoly of the presidency; "waving the bloody shirt" no longer insured success at the polls. Slavery and reconstruction were through as annual message headliners; new questions arising out of America's status as an industrial giant clamored for presidential attention. But the years from 1861 to 1884 had not been "bad"—if you relied for your information on the same reporter as did Congress annually. The dark, overcast skies of the 1850s had made the Presidents' search for silver lined clouds difficult but not impossible. The Republican chief executives with the exception of Johnson proved their mettle also in keeping their annual messages well insulated from contemporary difficulties. Even civil war and recriminations over reconstruction could not shake their official confidence.

Lincoln could scarcely avoid giving recognition to the agitating problems of his administration but the story as told in his annual messages certainly did not reveal the desperation of the national situation. He admitted, for example, in 1861 that the country was "in the midst of unprecedented political troubles," but he did not mention the military reverses of that disappointing year for the union forces. His brief reference to war related only to federal successes which he said, "demonstrate that the cause of the Union is advancing steadily and certainly southward."

By 1862 the President was able to see the "bright side" of foreign affairs, reporting: "If the conditions of our relations with other nations is less gratifying than it has usually been at former periods, it is certainly more satisfactory than a nation so unhappily distracted as we are might reasonably have apprehended." Not even the intervention of the French in Mexico and the continued use of French and British shipyards to build Confederate war vessels dampened the President's assurance in 1863 that "we remain in peace and friendship with foreign powers."

Johnson's sharp tongued reports "told all." His picture of the "state of the union" in 1867 was not pleasant: "It is well and publicly known that enormous frauds have been perpetrated on the Treasury and that colossal fortunes have been made at the public expense. This species of corruption has increased, is increasing, and if not diminished will soon bring us into total ruin and disgrace."[23]

In no uncertain terms Johnson raised the specter of race violence which he expected to follow in the wake of congressional reconstruction:

"The great difference between the two races in physical, mental and moral characteristics will prevent an amalgamation or fusion of them together in one homogeneous mass. If the inferior obtains the ascendency over the other, it will govern with reference only to its own interests . . . and create such a tyranny as this continent has never yet witnessed. . . . Of all the dangers which our nation has yet encountered, none are equal to those which must result from the success of the effort now making to Africanize the half of our country."[29]

In December, 1868, Johnson added to the indictment. Yet only a year later Grant reported quite a contrasting view: "We are blessed with peace at home, . . . with a territory unsurpassed in fertility . . . with a population of 40,000,000 free people, . . . with institutions closing to none the avenues to fame . . . or fortune . . . with freedom of the pulpit, the press, and the school; with a revenue flowing into the National Treasury beyond the requirements of the Government."[30]

The differences in the "states of the unions" were more in the beholder than in the beholden; orientation and purpose tinted the magnifying glass. As in earlier periods, a disaster might force a reluctant President to let a realistic appraisal enter the message. Grant, for example, referred to the "Panic of 1873" when he noted that "In the midst of great national prosperity a financial crisis has occurred that has brought low fortunes of gigantic proportions." This, however, was the exception; the rule was that contemporary affairs were treated in the superlative when possible, and minimized as temporary when the national condition could not support unalloyed optimism. Grant's admission that, "From the fall of Adam . . . to the present day no nation has ever been free from threatened danger to its prosperity and happiness"[31] was unique for its momentary lapse from the ritualistic belief expressed by the Presidents in the inevitablity of American progress.

Hayes and Arthur restored the reassuring complacency which had characterized the annual messages almost completely before 1830, and prevalently until the 1850s. Johnson's personal excursion from the dignified calm of the yearly report was no more than a memory and all indications were that henceforth the Presidents would be better behaved. All was quiet along the Potomac.

The literary style made a come back with Lincoln and Johnson who needing public support in their roles as strong executives, utilized striking phraseology and appeals to emotion. This was especially true of Lincoln who reserved for his annual messages some of his most eloquent writing. He refused to clutter the report with summations, leaving himself freer to concentrate on the public examination of crucial issues. In clear, convincing, heartfelt exposition, he earnestly pleaded the cause of moderation. He never forgot that he was one with those he led; he avoided the ornate, preferring instead a simplicity of expression which carried conviction. A much quoted paragraph is the one which concluded his appeal in 1862 for the adoption of the compensated emancipation amendment:

"Fellow-citizens, *we* can not escape history. We of this Congress and this administration will be remembered in spite of ourselves. No personal significance or insignificance can spare one or another of us. The fiery trial through which we pass will light us down in honor or dishonor to the latest generation. We *say* we are for the Union. The world will not forget that we say this. We know how to save the Union. The world knows we do know how to save it. We, even *we here* hold the power and bear the responsibility. In *giving* freedom to the *slave* we *assure* freedom to the *free*—honorable alike in what we give and what we preserve. We shall nobly save or meanly lose the last best hope of earth. Other means may succeed; this could not fail. The way is plain, peaceful, generous, just—a way which followed the world will forever applaud and God must forever bless."[32]

Informality made its first appearance in 1861—a very brief intrusion in Lincoln's first annual message. Then it disappeared again out of sight until the twentieth century. Referring to the appointment of General McClellan as Chief of the Army, Lincoln expressed the hope that the nation would give its full confidence to the new military leader. He illustrated the importance of doing this by making two observations: "It has been said that one bad general is better than two good ones, and the saying is true if taken to mean no more than that an army is better directed by a single mind, though inferior, than by two superior ones at variance and cross-purpose with each other. And the same is true in all joint operations wherein those engaged *can* have none but a common end in view and *can* differ only as to the choice of means. In a storm at sea no one on board *can* wish the ship to sink, and yet not unfrequently all go down together because too many will direct and no single mind can be allowed to control."[33]

Grant made an unique personal defense in his final message. The bitterness which had moved him to complain in his second inaugural address that "I have been the subject of abuse and slander scarcely ever equaled in political history" obviously lingered in his memory. He welcomed the opportunity afforded by his 1876 message to explain his position to the American people and, perhaps even more, to the historians who would evaluate his administration: "It was my fortune, or misfortune, to be called to the office of Chief Executive without any previous political training. From the age of 17 I had never even witnessed the excitement attending a Presidential campaign but twice antecedent to my own candidacy, and at but one of them was I eligible as a voter." [34]

Admitting that, "as all can see," errors had been made, Grant placed more of the blame on the shoulders of Congress because his assistants were, he said, "in nearly every case selected without a personal acquaintance with the appointee, but upon recommendations of the representatives chosen directly by the people." Under such circumstances, he continued, mistakes were bound to happen and no administration since Washington had been free from error. [35] He used the concluding pages to vindicate his continued recommendation for the annexation of Santo Domingo, and to append to this final annual message "a synopsis of administrative events and of all recommendations made by me during the last seven years."

Some increased flexibility in message content resulted from the growing practice of quoting other than executive sources. Before the 1860s, it was not unusual to find in the annual message quoted extracts from department reports, earlier presidential messages, official documents, and the Constitution. It was a distinct innovation, however, when Johnson bolstered his arguments on the currency issue by quoting from a source identified only as "one of our profound and most gifted statesman." Similarly unusual was Grant's quoting of "the greatest living British authority" in his discussion of a maritime dispute with England. Hayes' comment that he had asked the chairman of the Civil Service Commission to make a study of the British system, and his subsequent reference to this study, were also exceptional items. The idea that the United States could benefit from examining procedures in other countries was one that had not been reported by earlier Presidents.

From Lincoln to Arthur religious thanksgiving in the messages began to lag. It had been an accepted part of practically every "state of the union" report since 1790 but it began to show signs of disappearing gradually in the post-Civil War years.   Lincoln subscribed to the custom in all of his annual messages but without the florid embellishment which characterized an earlier generation's writing.   The opening sentence in 1863 was typical: "Another year of health and sufficiently abundant harvests has passed.   For these, and especially for the improved condition of our national affairs, our renewed and profoundest gratitude to God is due." Johnson continued the tradition is his first two messages; the first specifically accepted the custom: "To express gratitude to God in the name of the people for the preservation of the United States is my first duty in addressing you."   His third message made no religious mention, however, and only passing slight reference was included in his final report.

Grant restored the usual religious phrases to their customary place in his first four annual messages; but with equal consistency and greater inexplicability included no religious sentiments at all in his last four.   Hayes reversed the process; his "devout gratitude to the bountiful Giver of All Good" was reminiscent of the pre-1861 messages.   Arthur apparently was not completely impressed by the regulatory with which Hayes included religious thanksgiving in all of his messages; his first annual report commenced with an acknowledgment of divine help, the second left it until the last paragraph, and the last two omitted it completely.   By 1884 the status of this particular feature was clearly in doubt.   No less an authority than George Bancroft had recognized a change in the times when, in revising his histories in the early 1880s, he included appreciably fewer references to the intervention of "divine Providence"—a concession, according to his biographer, "to the changed temper of a less God-conscious public."[36]   The influence of Darwinism and the optimistic nineteenth century philosophy of automatic progress seemed to diminish the need for religious thanksgiving.   The Presidents were not alone in being poor prophets.

Chapter Five

RISE AND FALL OF THE PONDEROUS MESSAGE

Grover Cleveland was the first Democratic President after 1861. As mayor of Buffalo and governor of New York, he had established a reputation for dedication to "clean government" and thoroughness as an executive. He saw the role of government as the mediator of conflicting interests; a view which was expressed in his reverence for the separation of powers doctrine.

In his first inaugural address Cleveland pledged himself "to be guided by a just and unstrained construction of the Constitution." He spelled out this position in his first annual message in 1885: " . . . it is well for us bear in mind that our usefulness to the people's interests will be promoted by a constant appreciation of the scope and character of our respective duties as they relate to Federal legislation. While the Executive may recommend such measures as he shall deem expedient, the responsibility for legislative action must and should remain upon those selected by the people to make their laws."[1]

Cleveland's devotion to the system of checks and balances and his hostility to that wing of the Democratic party which held to Jacksonian principles weakened his leadership. He accepted a limited scope for the exercise of presidential power and thus, in spite of his vigorous actions within this area, left the presidency in 1897 at a low point in prestige. His designation by some as the most distinguished President between Lincoln and Theodore Roosevelt is based more on his success in negating bad legislation than his achievement in passing positive measures.[2]

He approached conscientiously the duty to present an annual message; his first document of almost 20,000 words exceeded in length all previous ones. The form followed the main outlines of the customary message: a systematic survey of foreign affairs came first, followed by a very detailed Treasury report, a summation of departmental operations, and the usual pledge of co-operation to work with Congress. Cleveland favored the practice of selecting one or two issues for particularized examination and argumentation leaving other matters for mere survey treatment. The items singled out for scrutinization were invariably of an economic nature; his first message, for example, emphasized the necessity for tariff reduction and strict avoidance of a Treasury surplus.

When the money continued to roll into the federal coffers and Congress refused to cut tariff rates, Cleveland wanted to make this condition the main issue of the 1888 election. The opening shot in his campaign came when he broke with all precedent and concentrated his entire 1887 "state of the union" message on a single subject: the tariff. His reasoning was based on the belief that this innovation "being an absolutely new departure, would in itself focus the attention of the country and cause comment and discussion of the issue which he was so urgently recommending."[3] This was indeed a "new departure" and signified that the message need not be a routine obligation for an executive who was venturesome.

Acknowledging that it had been the custom to present a resume of the general conditions of the country and to relate in some detail the operation of particular executive departments, Cleveland explained: "It would be especially agreeable to follow this course at the present time and to call attention to the valuable accomplishments of these Departments during the last fiscal year; but I am so much impressed with the paramount importance of the subject to which this communication has thus far been devoted that I shall forego the addition of any other topic, and only urge upon your immediate consideration the 'state of the union' as shown in the present condition of our Treasury and our general fiscal situation, upon which every element of our safety and prosperity depends."[4]

Cleveland rejected the charge that he favored "free trade" and refused to discuss the theories of the issue which he felt "savors too much of bandying epithets." He insisted that "It is a *condition* which confronts us, not a theory." He called for a reduction in taxes to a level necessary for an economical operation of the government, and restoration to the business of the country the "money which we hold in the Treasury through the perversion of governmental powers." The message concluded with the reminder that departmental reports submitted to Congress along with his annual report, "contain full and explicit information touching the transaction of the business intrusted to them and such recommendations relating to legislation in the public interest as they deem advisable." Since there was no provision for a report from the Secretary of State, Cleveland promised that a future communication "would acquaint Congress with the transactions of that important Department." The President failed in having his recommendations carried out; but he succeeded in calling the tariff issue sharply to public attention and forced his own party to espouse tariff reform in the election.

Benjamin Harrison who took over the presidency in 1889 was in complete harmony, both by temperament and political philosophy, with the doctrine of congressional supremacy held dear by his Republican party. In his opinion it was the duty of the President to make recommendations, but it was a duty which he held in common with others. The opening paragraph of his first annual message explained: "There are very few transactions in the administration of the Government that are even temporarily held in the confidence of those charged with the conduct of the public business. Every step taken is under the observation of an intelligent and watchful people. The state of the Union is known from day to day, and suggestions as to needed legislation find an earlier voice than that which speaks in these annual communications of the President to Congress."[5]

Harrison was content to devote most of his messages to a comprehensive but relaxed summation of executive actions; missing were the lectures and polemics which had made Cleveland's documents stimulating and provocative. In clear, concise, straightforward exposition, Harrison presented the pertinent facts and generally avoided excursions into the realm of observations, policies, or immoderate references to Congress or anyone else. Nevertheless, his messages continued the trend toward increased length; this, in spite, of the fact that greater emphasis was being placed on separate departmental reports to give information to Congress. Harrison explained it in this way in 1890: "The reports of the several Executive Departments, which will be laid before Congress in the usual course, will exhibit in detail the operations of the Government for the last fiscal year. Only the more important incidents and results, chiefly as may be the foundation of the recommendations I shall submit, will be referred to in this annual message."[6]

Sandwiched between Cleveland's two terms, the Harrison administration offered a message content similar in nature but not in emphasis. Development in the West won special notice: the opening of Oklahoma Territory to settlers and the almost over-night growth of Oklahoma City and Guthrie; the admission of four new states— South Dakota, North Dakota, Montana, and Washington; and in 1892, referring to the most advantageous placement of the U.S. Army, Harrison suggested that "The new posts should have the proper strategic relations to the only 'frontiers' we now have—those of the seacoast and of our northern and part of our southern boundary."

With regard to foreign affairs Harrison reported on differences with Germany and England over Samoa, with England over the seal fisheries in the Bering Sea, and with Chile over incidents related to the *Baltimore* fracas. All were peacefully adjusted, allowing the President to state in 1892 that "Our relations with other nations are now undisturbed by any serious controversy." There had been trouble in 1891 when eleven persons, three of them Italian nationals, were lynched by a New Orleans mob. This incident, reported by Harrison as being "most deplorable and discreditable," constituted America's first major controversy with Italy. More typical of the times, however, were the President's references, in 1892, to the First International American Conference and to a meeting of maritime nations to revise and amend the rules and regulations governing vessels at sea. Both assemblies were then meeting in Washington. The United States was on the threshold of a more active participation in international gatherings.

In 1893 Cleveland was back in office. His annual message promised "to abridge this communication as much as is consistent with its purpose" by making only such references as were not included in the departmental reports. It and the next year's message were like other Cleveland ones but in 1895 he reverted as in 1887 to a focused message. After noting that the departmental reports "fully and plainly exhibit what has been accomplished within the scope of their respective duties, the President commented: "I therefore deem my executive duty adequately performed at this time by presenting to the Congress the important phases of our situation as related to our intercourse with foreign nations and a statement of the financial problems which confront us, omitting, except as they are related to these topics, any reference to departmental operations."[3]

The multiplying activities of the executive department and the painstaking care with which Cleveland reported on the "state of the union" led him to make a critical appraisal of his method and to suggest a partial means of reform in his final message: "To secure brevity and avoid tiresome narration I shall omit many details concerning matters within Federal control which, though by no means unimportant, are more profitably discussed in departmental reports. I shall also further curtail this communication by omitting a minute recital of many minor incidents connected with our foreign relations which have heretofore found a place in Executive messages, but are now contained in a report of the Secretary of State, which is herewith submitted."[9]

However, the communication which followed consumed more than 14,000 words; the attempt to curtail the foreign affairs section suffered because of the many references which were needed to report on the country's emerging status as a world power.

The content of the Cleveland messages reflected a time when the United States was in the throes of transformation from a basically agricultural economy to a predominently industrial one, the while it was groping toward an expansionist policy. His outright opposition to imperialism was set forth in his very first message in 1885: "I do not favor a policy of acquisition of new and distant territories or the incorporation of remote interests with our own." His fixed resistance to the annexation of Hawaii, intervention in Cuba, and similar ventures was defended in massive argumentation throughout all his reports to Congress. The dispute with Great Britain regarding the Venezuelan-British Guiana boundary which Cleveland considered an American question under his interpretation of the Monroe Doctrine was discussed yearly, culminating in his announcement in 1896 of the United States-British agreement to arbitrate the issue.

The tariff question was a hardy Cleveland perennial. Echoed over and over again was his statement in 1885: "Our revenues are in excess of the actual needs of an economical administration of the Government justifying a reduction in the amount exacted from the people for its support." With equal tenacity, he argued for the maintenance of a gold standard giving over the bulk of his 1895 message to an examination of this issue which paralleled his inspection of the tariff problem eight years earlier.[10]

Cleveland's determination to prevent raids by war veterans on the public treasury was emphasized: "The laxity of ideas prevailing among a large number of our people regarding pensions is becoming every day more marked." He proposed a careful scrutiny and tightening of pension awards. A champion of civil service reform, the President talked incessantly about the need for good public officials and reported with great satisfaction the progress which he felt was being made in securing better qualified people. Recurring issues commanded as usual the chief executive's notice: the year 1895 was reported as being free from Indian disturbances "and the chances of further depredations on their part are constantly becoming more remote and improbable"; the pesky Mormon mores were commented upon and it was optimistically claimed that "the forbidden practice of polygamy within the United States is virtually at an end;" and homesteading was favored as opposed to the accumulation of a large area of the public lands "directly or through fraud, in the hands of a single individual." Labor and capital became familiar subject entries; in his final message Cleveland urged the people to take a deep interest in the doings of trusts and monopolies.

A brief mention of "occurrences of a deeply regrettable nature" and the "painful but imperative duty to obtain . . . a new personal channel of diplomatic intercourse" with Great Britain was the President's polite reference to the famous "Sackville-West letter" episode in 1888 and the political blunder which probably cost Cleveland the election that year.

The inauguration of William McKinley ushered in a gradual swing away from congressional dominance toward greater balance between executive and legislative branches. His long experience in Congress equipped him to deal with that body, and the United States' entrance into world affairs on a large scale strengthened the importance of the presidency. Wilfred E. Binkley contends that "Not since the presidency of Thomas Jefferson, had there been achieved such an integration of the political branches of the federal government and such consequent coherence and sense of direction in the functioning."[11]

President McKinley's four annual messages were concerned predominately with the approaching crisis in Cuba, the Spanish-American War, and the subsequent ramifications of the Treaty of Paris. Domestic reporting was limited to only a few issues of transcendent importance and these were treated in relatively slight detail. His first message in 1897, for example, devoted a large section to an analysis of the Cuban revolt concluding with this comment: "I am forced by the length of this Message to omit many important references to affairs of the Government with which Congress will have to deal at the present session. They are fully discussed in the departmental reports, to all of which I invite your earnest attention."

A year later the military phase of the Spanish-American War was over and the President traced the steps which had led to the conflict; a "brief recital of its more salient features" followed for over 7,000 words. Congress was again urged to rely on departmental reports while the President informed on the "state of the union" by

surveying in a detailed way United States relations with its possessions and some foreign countries. In 1900 he included, verbatim,
the instructions which he had issued to a commission organized
to establish civil government in the Philippines. This reference
alone was longer than Washington's first annual address.

McKinley obviously was not interested in presenting a balanced
report; foreign affairs dominated. The comprehensive approach
was still favored and the messages mushroomed to an average length
of 20,000 words. This size did not make for popular reading and
definitely interfered with the President's effectiveness in getting
his point-of-view across to the public. There is probably the usual
amount of truth in Peter Finley Dunne's lampooning of one Mc-
Kinley annual message:

"Did ye r-read th' prisidint's message?" asked Mr. Dooley.

"I did not," said Mr. Hennessy.

"Well, ye-re r-right," said the philosopher. "I didn't mesilf. 'Tis
manny years since I give up my devotion to that form iv fiction.
I don't think anny wan r-reads a message but th' clerk iv th' house iv
riprisintatives, an' he has to hold his job."[12]

The content of the McKinley annual messages revealed that the
singular calm in which foreign affairs lay in the 1880s was past. By
the late 1890s Cleveland's curbing of the "large policy" in the
Caribbean and Far East had been overcome by a President who
chose to ride a wave of popular sentiment favoring expansion. In
1897, after reviewing in detail the revolutions in Cuba against the
Spanish, he concluded with this warning: "If it shall hereafter
appear to be a duty imposed by our obligations to ourselves, to
civilization and humanity to intervene with force, it shall be without
fault on our part and only because the necessity for such action will
be so clear as to command the support and approval of the civilized
world."[13]

A year later the "splendid little war" was over and the President
applauded the armed forces, particularly Commodore Simpson's
defeat of the Spanish at Santiago, an "astounding victory for which
neither ancient nor modern history affords a parallel." Symbolic
of the times was the recommendation that a standing appropriation
be made for United States representatives at international confer-
ences because "Hardly a year passes that this government is not
invited to national participation at some important foreign center."
In 1899 McKinley gave over much of his message to a report on the
growing overseas American holdings: the Philippines, Hawaii,

Alaska, and Puerto Rico. Features of the 1900 report were a narration of the difficulties related to the Boxer Rebellion in China, a restatement of the "Open Door" policy, an admission of the necessity for keeping "considerable forces in the Philippines for some time to come," and, of melancholy interest, a reference to the approaching Pan-American Exposition which was destined to be the site of McKinley's fatal wounding.

The leadership exercised by McKinley under the pressure of war and foreign expansion was seized by Theodore Roosevelt; he fashioned it into a positive instrument complete with rationalization and justification for its use at home and abroad. Without apology he rejected the Republican theory of congressional supremacy, substituting the view that the executive "was a steward of the people bound actively and affirmatively to do all he could for the people, and not to content himself with the negative merit of keeping his talents undamaged in a napkin. . . . My belief was that it was not only his right but his duty to do anything that the needs of the Nation demanded unless such action was forbidden by the Constitution or by the laws. Under this interpretation . . . I did and caused to be done many things not previously done by the President . . . I did not usurp power, but I did greatly broaden the use of executive power. . . . I acted for the public welfare, I acted for the common well-being of all our people."[14]

Roosevelt made it clear that as President he would take the initiative in the lawmaking process. Never before had any chief executive so openly asserted this prerogative. All of the preceding Presidents had been careful to avoid any appearance of "dictating" to Congress; the few who made their opinions felt did so by virtue of their influence in Congress and not by bridging the gap between the separated powers. The position that the President is the servant of Congress rather than the people was labedel by T.R. as the "Buchanan view" of the presidency; one which Roosevelt felt was "narrowly legalistic" and usually held by most able lawyers who were past middle age, well-meaning, respectable citizens. Writing in 1913, T.R. left no doubt as to what had been his concept of the presidency:

"In theory the Executive has nothing to do with legislation. In practice, as things are now, the Executive is or ought to be peculiarly representative of the people as a whole. As often as not the action of the Executive offers the only means by which the people can get

the legislation they demand and ought to have.   Therefore a good
executive under the present condition of American political life
must take a very active interest in getting the right kind of legislation, in addition to performing his executive duties with an eye
single to the public welfare.   More than half of my work as Governor
was in the direction of getting needed and important legislation.
I accomplished this only by arousing the people, and riveting their
attention on what was done."[15]

Armed with this self-proclaimed duty to lead T.R., in his own
words, found "the White House is a bully pulpit."   The President
was interested in everything and had a ready opinion and quotable
observation on every subject.   All of his annual messages, except
the second, were among the longest ever delivered; his last four
all exceeded 23,000 words each.

Since the positive government Roosevelt advocated must attract
attention to be successful, he was quick to utilize any means by
which he could achieve his goals.   The annual message fitted naturally
into his arsenal.   Addressed to Congress in form only, T.R. more
than any of his predecessors aimed his report at the American and
world audience.   Any pretense of supplying merely factual information for the guidance of Congress was dropped.   In its place, Roosevelt
substituted short essay-type commentaries on a multitude of subjects.
These sermons supplied the reader with the background of the
issue, the resultant problem, and the proposed presidential solution.
Any one of these "essays" could have served conveniently and adequately as a separate speech on a specific topic.   The complete
message added up to a very readable, stimulating, highly partisan,
personalized document, but the formidable length discouraged any
but piecemeal digestion.

Roosevelt's supreme confidence in himself and his program were
underlined on every page.   The messages were replete with argumentation and pronouncements.   His third message, for example,
contained a masterful presentation of developments preceding the
Panama Revolution, the steps taken by the President, a lengthy
statistical survey showing the number of revolutions, rebellions, in-
surrections, riots, and other outbreaks in the previous fifty-seven
years, and a final conclusion that under the circumstances "the
United States would have been guilty of folly and weakness, amount-
ing in their sum to a crime against the Nation, had it acted otherwise
than it did when the revolution of November 3 last took place in
Panama."

No issue was too large for T.R. to tackle and very few were small enough to elude his comment. In the same message in which he proclaimed what came to be known as the "Roosevelt Corollary to the Monroe Doctrine," he lectured on the necessity of inflicting corporal punishment on certain offenders like wife-beaters.[16]

Roosevelt had a flare for the dramatic and his enthusiasm was contagious. Some say his chief contribution to the progressive cause was to vitalize it as well as make it respectable. The need for conservation, for example, was explained in this way: "Optimism is a good characteristic, but if carried to an excess becomes foolishness. We are prone to speak of the resources of this country as inexhaustible; this is not so. The mineral wealth of the country, the coal, iron, oil, gas, and the like, does not reproduce itself, and therefore is certain to be exhausted ultimately; and wastefulness in dealing with it today means that our descendants will feel the exhaustion a generation or two before they otherwise would."[17]

The logic of "either-or" appealed to T.R. and he sprinkled it throughout his messages. In urging an ever increasing navy he offered these alternatives: "The American people must either build and maintain an adequate navy or make up their minds definitely to accept a secondary position in international affairs. It has been well said that there is no surer way of courting national disaster than to be 'opulent, aggressive, and unarmed.' "[18]

To the American people, he offered alternatives of "greatness": " . . . for woe or for weal, our place must be great among nations. We may either fail greatly or succeed greatly; but we can not avoid the endeavor from which either great failure or great success must come."[19] Concerning immigration, he stated the proposition simply: "We can not have too much immigration of the right kind, and we should have none at all of the wrong kind."[20] Misdeeds and corruption were a favorite target, bringing forth a blast of righteous indignation and wrath. Exaggeration, bombast, and over simplification were not ruled out when Roosevelt was in hot pursuit of a "deadly sin." For example, he charged, "There can be no crime more serious than bribery. . . .   The givers and takers of bribes stand on an evil preeminence of infamy."[21]

Literally hundreds of recommendations poured forth. Some were even clearly outside federal jurisdiction. In the case of child labor, for example, Roosevelt admitted the problem could be met, in most cases, only by the states themselves, but he favored having the national government compile "comprehensive information as to the conditions of labor of children in the different States" on the grounds that the investigation and publication of this material "would tend toward the securing of approximately uniform legislation of the proper character among the several States."[22]   In his annual messages domestic issues forced foreign affairs into a balance; a shift in emphasis which was in harmony with the progressive movement.   New subjects jostled old ones introducing problem areas never before touched on by a President.   In his first "time at bat" in 1901, Roosevelt proposed, among other things: giving federal courts jurisdiction over anyone who kills or attempts to kill the President, government inspection and examination of the workings of corporations engaged in inter-state commerce, creation of a Department of Commerce and Industries, re-enactment and strengthening of the Chinese exclusion law, application of the principle of reciprocity in tariff scheduling, increased federal action in the conservation of natural resources, continued building of the Navy, extension of the merit system, recognition of the Indian as an individual and not just as a member of a tribe, and generous appropriations for the Smithsonian Institution and the Library of Congress.[23]

The seven Roosevelt messages which followed brought an accleration rather than an abatement in the volume of suggestions, observations, pronouncements, and recommendations.   T.R. was equally voluble in discussing foreign affairs.   His "speak softly and carry a big stick" philosophy was in evidence although "speak softly" often seemed a description of dubious application.   Lectures on international rectitude went hand in hand with itemized reporting: "Peace is normally a great good, and normally it coincides with righteousness; but it is righteousness and not peace which should bind the conscience of a nation. . . .   A just war is in the long run far better for a nation's soul than the most prosperous peace obtained by the acquiscence in wrong or injustice."[24]

Central to T.R.'s foreign affairs reporting was his reiterated belief that "The Monroe Doctrine should be treated as the cardinal feature of American foreign policy."   His interpretation of the Doctrine in his 1901 message that "We do not guarantee any state against punishment if it misconducts itself, . . . " underwent a famous metamorphosis from one of non-intervention by any European power to one of intervention by the United States when he announced in 1904 the so-called "Roosevelt Corollary" which cast the United States in the role of exerciser of an "international police power" against any American states guilty of "flagrant, chronic wrongdoing or impotence."[25]

In 1908 Roosevelt changed the format of his final message; he used headings to introduce each subject area. The system had been tried by Grant and abandoned by him, but now it was welcomed back because of the message's great length. With the fragmentation of the document into topic categories, the over-all coherence suffered; now there was a thinly connected string of individual reports in which the subjects could have been reshuffled without damage to internal structure and readability. Unfortunately—or fortunately, according to one's viewpoint—it was this insistence on having his complete say which hampered T.R.'s effectiveness. Norman Small feels that Roosevelt's recommendations were too numerous, not specific enough, and that Congress and the public were not keenly alert to his proposals because the recommendations were "frequently obscured by the injection of lengthy discourses upon the moral rectitude of the Executive's activities or upon subjects not susceptible to legislation by the Federal government."[26]

William Howard Taft did not follow in the foot-steps of his illustrious predecessor. He rejected Roosevelt's "stewardship" theory stressing instead the restrictions on presidential power. Writing in 1916, he contended that "the President can exercise no power which cannot be fairly and reasonably traced to some specific grant of power or justly implied and included within such express grant as necessary and proper to its exercise. Such specific grant must be either in the Federal Constitution or in an act of Congress passed in pursuance thereof. There is no undefined residum of power which he can exercise because it seems to him to be in the public interest."[27]

Taft's relationship with Congress was more formal and deferential; legislative initiative passed once again from the White House to the Capitol. The doctrine of "separation of powers" showed its deep-rooted acceptance and its recuperative ability. The switch from Roosevelt to Taft was characterized by one commentator as like changing from an automobile to a horsedrawn carriage. The new series of annual messages were quiet, factual, dispassionate, scholarly reports of the "state paper" variety. Taft used a heading breakdown based on departments rather than subjects; the emphasis was on giving Congress complete information with a minimum of personal observations. His first annual message explained the reason for his detailed description of State Department transactions: "there is no provision either by statute or custom for a formal report by the Secretary of State to the President or to Congress, and a Presidential message is the only means by which the condition of our foreign affairs is brought to the attention of Congress and the public."

In domestic reporting, Taft said that he would follow the now firmly established course of relying on department summations to inform Congress: "I shall touch only those matters which seem to me to call for special mention on my part without minimizing in any way the recommendations made by them for legislation affecting their respective Departments, in all of which I wish to express my general concurrence."

Taft's attention to detail was such, however, that it did not allow him to curtail the message substantially. When his second one soared to an unprecedented length of over 30,000 words, it was evident that the message was too unwieldy and threatened to defeat its original function of providing a convenient overview and analysis of the "state of the union." Taft recognized this condition and in 1911 he split the annual communication into a series of four messages; the last of which was sent sixteen days after the first.[28] He explained in his introductory remarks that the number of important subjects calling for executive comment and the transmission of exhaustive reports of special commissions "make it impossible to include in one message of reasonable length a discussion of the topics that ought to be brought to the attention of the National Legislature at its first regular session."

The serial version of the "state of the union" was hailed editorially by the *New York Tribune*: "In presenting his annual message to Congress in parts, each devoted to a single subject, President Taft makes a useful break in a custom which was becoming burdensome. President's messages, with the importance and complexity of the topics treated in them, had grown too long for the public to read. . . . The points which the President wishes to make, presented separately, will have an opportunity to produce the desired impression. The public will have time to consider and discuss each by itself. Mr. Taft's discussion of the trust problem gains by being thus presented to the people. Attention centers upon it and it is not drawn away by the counter question of say, the tariff question or any other of the multitudinous considerations ordinarily put forth at once by a President performing his constitutional duty of informing Congress regarding national affairs."[29]

In 1912 Taft again split his message into separate sections, this time into three. His yearly reports were able, thorough documents but, crammed with statistics, they lacked the vigor of expression which distinguished the goading messages of Cleveland and Theodore Roosevelt. Slow and deliberate, Taft was unsurpassed in his reverence for the Constitution and in his respect for the orderly process of law—"admirable characteristics but not popularly exciting after Rooseveltian fireworks." [30] The Taft messages are the high water mark of the all-encompassing, carefully documented, conscientiously prepared "state of the union" reviews. [31] He respected "expertness" in government and was a great believer in "impartial scientific study" preliminary to legislation—the commission approach. The results of these studies were duly (and dully) reported. He also displayed his penchant for economy in government wherever he could in the annual messages although not usually as bluntly as when he recommended that certain navy-yards be abolished: "With a fleet considerably less than half the size of that of the British navy, we have ship-yards more than double the number." Of special interest to students of political science was Taft's recommendation in 1912 that the heads of the executive department should have seats in each House so they could take part in discussions and answer questions. Nothing came of his suggestion; the American system remained without a parliamentary-type "Question Time."

In foreign affairs something of a "lull before the storm" was in effect; Taft reported with pride that the seventy year old fisheries dispute with Great Britain had been submitted to the Permanent Court of Arbitration at the Hague for settlement: "the first case involving such great international questions." The encouragement of diplomatic-commercial ventures in foreign countries was a Taft policy; in 1910, he reported the actions of a "group of American bankers [who] undertook . . . to advance funds for railways and other improvements contributing directly to [Honduras'] prosperity and commerce—an arrangement long desired by this Government."

For the most part satisfaction with contemporary conditions and confidence in the future development of the American system remained a trademark of the annual messages from Cleveland to Taft. Admissions of weakness were invariably coupled with compensating claims of strength. Harrison's remarks in 1892 are typical of the "best of all possible worlds" philosophy of Presidents: "If any are discontented with their state here, if any believe that wages or

prices, the return for honest toil, are inadequate, they should not fail
to remember that there is no other country in the world where the
conditions that seem to them hard would not be accepted as highly
prosperous. The English agriculturist would be glad to exchange
the returns for his labor for those of the American farmer and the
Manchester workmen their wages for those of their fellows at Fall
River."[32]

Momentary lapses into pessimism did break through, however,
giving glimpses of presidential "righteous indignation." Cleveland
in 1888 after his defeat by Harrison made a scathing attack on the
voting record of Congress and the "selfish and private interests" which
he saw triumphing everywhere. He warned the lawmakers and the
public that "Communism is a hateful thing and a menace to peace
and organized government; but the communism of combined wealth
and capital, the outgrowth of overweening cupidity and selfishness,
which insidiously undermines the justice and integrity of free institutions, is not less dangerous than the communism of oppressed
poverty and toil, which, exasperated by injustice and discontent,
attacks with wild disorder the citadel of rule."[33]

The positive program Theodore Roosevelt favored could not move
forward based on satisfaction with the *status quo*. Desire for change
had to be nourished first by creating distaste for the current diet
and then providing new menus to excite the nation's dulled appetite.
T.R.'s messages paid dutiful tribute to the achievements of the past
but they did not minimize the shortcomings of the present. His
announced disdain for the "muckrakers" did not dissuade him from
capitalizing on the exposures they made and the predisposition for
change which their writings encouraged.

Roosevelt's road clearing approach of introducing reform measures
was a harbinger of the technique to be followed shortly by the
twentieth century Democratic Presidents. His call for public health
legislation provides an example of his manner of thrusting: "This
nation can not afford to lag behind in the world-wide battle now being
waged by all civilized people with the microscopic foes of mankind,
nor ought we longer to ignore the reproach that this Government
takes more pains to protect the lives of hogs and of cattle than of
human beings."[34]

The inclusion of religious thanksgiving in the messages between
1885 and 1912 was limited almost solely to those of McKinley.
He consistently acknowledged the active assistance of a "beneficient

Providence." In a grandiloquent style reminiscent of an earlier era, McKinley even made the unusual entry of religious mention in the body of a message when, after pridefully relating the military success of the Spanish-American War, he cautioned: "In tracing these events we are constantly reminded of our obligations to the Divine Master for His watchful care over us and His safe guidance, for which the nation makes reverent acknowledgment and offers humble prayer for the continuance of His favor."

Cleveland included no religious thanksgiving and made only passing reference in one message to the work which "God has given the American people to do." Harrison and Taft maintained a completely secular tone; T.R. made one formal mention of the obligation owed to Providence and hardly more than scant reference to an existing divinity. All of his yearly reports, however, fairly shone with a moralistic lacquer. Elihu Root accused Roosevelt of acting as if he had discovered the Ten Commandments and others noticed his habit of seeing all questions as moral issues. Roosevelt's analysis of the actions he had taken is illustrative: "This Nation's foreign policy is based on the theory that right must be done between nations precisely as between individuals, and in our actions for the last ten years we have in this matter proven our faith by our deeds. We have behaved, and are behaving, towards other nations as in private life an honorable man would behave towards his fellows."[35]

The influence of Darwinism was not lost on the Presidents. McKinley, for example in 1899, reporting on the proposed participation of the United States at a World Exposition, noted the application of the "theory" to social affairs: "In this age of keen rivalry among the nations for mastery in commerce, the doctrine of evolution and the rule of the survival of the fittest must be as inexorable in their operations as they are positive in the results they bring about. The place won in the struggle by an industrial people can only be held by an unrelaxed endeavor and constant advance in achiement."[36]

A favorite Roosevelt figure of speech related to the ebb and flow in nature with always the same conclusion: "The wave will recede; but the tide will advance." Such were the sentiments of the leader and the lead as they moved confidently into the "brave new world" of the twentieth century.

Chapter Six

RENASCENCE OF THE SPEECH FROM THE WHITE HOUSE

In 1908 Woodrow Wilson, then president of Princeton University and one of the nation's outstanding political scientists, delivered a series of lectures at Columbia University on the American presidency. The thesis of his appraisal was that the President would never again be just the domestic officer or the mere executive that he had been in the 1830s and 1840s but "must stand always at the front of our affairs, and the office will be as big and as influential as the man who occupies it."[1]

In the election of 1912 the "scholar in politics," though winning only 42% of the popular vote, piled up the largest electoral majority up to that time and was given the right to put his academic theories to work. Wilson was a Jeffersonian in his respect for the supremacy of legislative power in a democratic system but he did not subscribe to Jefferson's belief in the rigid separation of powers; in his view it was not only a right but a duty of the executive to guide the legislative process.[2] He was impressed with some features of the British parliamentary system and was both conversant and sympathetic with Theodore Roosevelt's "stewardship theory."

Shortly after his election Wilson made clear his concept of the President's role: "The President is expected by the nation to be the leader of his party, as well as the chief executive officer of the government, and the country will take no excuses from him. He must play the part and play it successfully, or lose the country's confidence. He must be the prime minister, as much concerned with the guidance of legislation as with the just and orderly execution of law, and he is the spokesman of the nation in everything, even in the most momentous and delicate dealings of the government in foreign affairs."[3]

To implement this closer co-operation between executive and legislative branches, Wilson re-established an old custom; on April 7, 1913, he announced that he would deliver in person his message at the commencement of the first (Special) session of the Sixty-Third Congress. He allowed himself to be quoted directly as to why he was doing so: "The reasons are very simple. I think that is the only dignified way for the President to address the Congress at the opening of the session. Instead of sending the address to be read perfunctorily in the Clerk's familiar tone of voice, I thought that the dignified and natural thing was to read it. It is a precedent which, it is true, has been discontinued for a long time, but which is a very respectable precedent."[4]

This decision was not sudden and on impulse. In 1889 Wilson, then a young student of the American constitutional system, had expressed dissatisfaction with the way in which the Presidents after John Adams delivered a written message to Congress. He complained that this form worked against the "foundation for a much more habitual and informal and yet at the same time much more public and responsible, interchange of opinions between Executive and Congress." Having been interpreted by some to "exclude the President from any but the most formal and ineffectual utterances of perfunctory advice," Wilson felt that the American chief executive "and legislature have been cut off from co-operation and mutual confidence to an extent with which no other modern system furnishes a parallel."[5]

His steadfast interest in the presidential message was indicated in his Columbia University lectures twenty years later. "Leadership in government naturally belongs to its executive officer," he argued, and he rejected the attitude of the Presidents who "have scrupulously refrained from attempting to determine either the subjects or the character of legislation," because of what Wilson considered a too literal interpretation of their duty: "The Constitution explicitly authorizes the President to recommend to Congress 'such measures as he shall deem necessary and expedient,' and it is not necessary to the integrity of even the literary theory of the Constitution to insist that such recommendations should be merely perfunctory, . . . A President's messages to Congress have no more weight or authority than their intrinsic reasonableness and importance give them; but that is their only constitutional limitation."[6]

He was impatient with Presidents who had not perceived that the duty to speak out was as clearly their right as the power to veto. He condemned the "timid fear" of some Presidents who seemed to feel that by their use of the power to recommend legislation, "they might offend some law of taste which had become a constitutional principle." With prophetic directness, in 1908, Wilson had focused on the presidential message as one of the instruments best suited to facilitate executive leadership. In the past, he argued, there have been periods "when the presidential messages were utterly without practical significance, perfunctory documents which few persons except the editors of newspapers took the trouble to read". However, "if the President has personal force and cares to exercise it, there is this tremendous difference between his messages and the views of any other citizen either outside Congress or in it; that the whole country reads them and feels the writer speaks with an authority and a responsibility which the people themselves have given him."[7]

In 1913 the ex-professor of political science was in a position to follow his own advice and give vitality to the annual message. Some of the President's cabinet were reported to be a "trifle shaky" about his decision to abandon the written message and appear before Congress in person.[8] On Capitol Hill, many members resented the change to an oral communication seeing in it a possible encroachment of the executive on the legislative body. The Senators, in particular, were disturbed with most of the opposition coming from the President's own party. Vice President Thomas Marshall rather than submit the usual request for unanimous consent to have the chief executive address Congress declared it a question of high privilege on which unanimous consent was not required. The *New York Times* headlined its news story: "President's Visit Nettles Senators; Some Democrats Resent His Plan to Deliver Oral Message to Congress Today; 'Like Speech from Throne'."[9]

Well informed on the difficulties occasioned by the congressional reply to the President which had followed each appearance by Washington and Adams, Wilson made it clear that he would expect "no formal answer from Congress except in the legislation which he [would] recommend." Thus, while the personal address was being resurrected, the practice of making replies which had been so odious to many early lawmakers was left entombed. The announcement that the President would appear in person naturally attracted large crowds to the Capitol. The galleries were filled to capacity and corridors outside were jammed with people trying in vain to gain admission. The floor of the House was similarly crowded, the entire membership of Congress having assembled to hear the President.

Wilson was accompanied by no private secretary or aide of any kind and the absence of pomp and circumstance was duly noted by the *New York Times*: " . . . the ceremonial, if it may be properly called that, was of the plainest character. There were no uniforms worn by those who sat on the floor, and the whole proceedings had about them an air of democratic simplicity."[10]

The President cushioned his opening remarks in a tactful attempt to assuage any congressional sensitivities: "I am very glad to have this opportunity to address the two Houses directly and to verify for myself the impression that the President of the United States is a person, not a mere department of the Government hailing Congress from some isolated island of jealous power, sending messages, not speaking naturally and with his own voice—that he is a human being trying to co-operate with other human beings in a common service. After this pleasant experience I shall feel quite normal in all our dealings with one another."[11]

The message dealt with the single topic of tariff reform; the attendant ceremony and speech itself took less than ten minutes. The *New York Times* detected no evidence of stage fright in Mr. Wilson's performance;[12] but then, he had been lecturing for a good many years.

The passing of a 112-year old political practice was greeted with mixed feelings. The *New York Times* was cautiously doubtful about the advantages of the new procedure but it did admit of some improvement: a spoken message was bound to be shorter and "If the day of long messages has passed the country is to be congratulated." The editorial concluded, "The wonder is that in seven years Theodore Roosevelt never thought of this way of stamping his personality upon his age."[13]

Ex-President Taft thought the innovation a good one because it fixed "the attention of the country on Congress and thus that of Congress on the recommendations of the President." He added: "I cannot refrain from a smile, however, when I think of the oratory which is lost because Mr. Roosevelt or I did not inaugurate such a change. The eloquence that would have resounded from the followers of Jefferson in denouncing a return to royal ceremony and the aping of the 'speech from the throne' can be supplied with little effort of the imagination."[14]

Convinced that popular support acting on a representative Congress was an essential bulwark to energetic and effective government, Wilson employed the annual message creatively as an instrument to give presidential direction and guidance. It was his great contribution to the presidency, says Wilfred E. Binkley, to have made the message to Congress "the basis of dynamic executive leadership. The extraordinary significance of the State of the Union message today owes much to [his] imagination and initiative."[15] He widened the focus enough to meet the obligation of reporting on the "state of the union" but he refused to present an omnium-gatherum in the format of the general, superficial review that most Presidents had felt it their duty to deliver. In his first annual address Wilson candidly stated his intention:

"I shall ask your indulgence if I venture to depart in some degree from the usual custom of setting before you in formal review the many matters which have engaged the attention and called for the action of the several departments of the Government . . . because the list is long, very long, and would suffer in the abbreviation to which I should have to subject it. I shall submit to you the reports of the heads of the several departments, in which these subjects are set forth in careful detail, and beg that they may receive the thoughtful attention of your committees and of all Members of the Congress who may have the leisure to study them. Their obvious importance, as constituting the very substance of the business of the Government, makes comment and emphasis on my part unnecessary."[16]

Other Presidents had made similar declarations of their desire to avoid tedius compendiums but none succeeded like Wilson. His message, terse and readable, took thirty minutes to deliver. In place of the usual multitudinous foreign affairs entries, the President made reference only to the Bryan Peace treaties and to his displeasure with the Huerta regime in Mexico. The domestic scene was surveyed in a limited way with the emphasis clearly on recommendations and policy proposals rather than on factual reporting. A year later Wilson supplied the professorial answer to his disinclination to dwell on past events: "I should like in this address to review the notable record [of the Sixty-Third Congress] and try to make adequate assessment of it; but no doubt we stand too near the work that has been done and are ourselves too much part of it to play the part of historians toward it. . . . Moreover, our thoughts are now more of the future than of the past."[17]

Wilson's form for the annual message followed function; each communication was designed to achieve certain specific objectives. No single pattern is discernable in the eight he delivered to Congress. The pressure of contemporary affairs and Wilson's desire to attract attention and get action, rather than consistency in presentation, dictated the style and content.

Wilson's 1914 report devoted about three-fourths of its text to a survey of legislative matters before the President said a "few words upon two topics, much discussed out of doors": government expenditures and national defense. Wilson was clearly speaking to the whole nation when he declared that "The country has been misinformed" by those who charge that the Government had been negligent of national defense. One year later, the President, in a communication reminiscent of Cleveland's tariff message of 1887, restricted his entire address to a single theme: "the thorough preparation of the nation to care for its own security and to . . . play the impartial role in this hemisphere and in the world which we all believe to have been providentially assigned to it."

In 1916 no reference was made to foreign affairs. Winner in that year's election, Wilson used the address to enumerate "some things left undone at the last session which there will now be time to complete and which it seems necessary in the interest of the public to do at once." Barely 2,000 words in length, the speech took nineteen minutes to read and was a total "neglect of duty" as far as reporting on the "state of the union" was concerned. Of course, the type of information formerly provided to Congress in the annual message was not totally lacking; Wilson very ably utilized special addresses to present a continuing appraisal of the nation's condition. His famous "Peace Without Victory" speech, for example, followed by one month the unimpressive 1916 annual message.

By December, 1917, the United States was a belligerent in World War I. Wilson in his message called for an immediate declaration of war against Austria-Hungary and reiterated America's war aims. His impatience with factual and statistical reporting was evident: "I shall not undertake to detail or even to summarize . . . events. The practical particulars of the part we have played in them [World War I] will be laid before you in the reports of the executive departments. I shall discuss only our present outlook upon these vast affairs, our present duties, and the immediate means of accomplishing the objects we shall hold always in view."[18]

A year later Wilson, though acknowledging that it was "too soon to assess" the results of the war, nevertheless allowed himself to play historian, explaining: "But some great outstanding facts are unmistakable and constitute, in a sense, part of the public business with which it is our duty to deal. To state them is to set the stage for the legislative and executive action which must grow out of them and which we have yet to shape and determine."[19]

The address, accordingly, departed from the usual Wilsonian emphasis on a spotlighted area of consideration, throwing its presidential beam instead over the entire domestic landscape. The congressional elections of 1918 had given the Republicans control of Congress and coming as it did after Wilson's personal appeal for the return of Democratic majorities, the results were interpreted as a repudiation of his leadership. He was no longer "prime minister"; a hostile and unco-operative Congress confronted him. Wilson had said in 1908 that "The chief weapon of the President in compelling Congress to follow his leadership is public opinion." In the Fall of 1919 he embarked on a 9,500 mile speaking tour of the West to make a direct report to the people in defense of the Versailles Treaty and the League of Nations. He suffered a physical collapse; a subsequent stroke prevented him from ever again appearing before Congress. Wilson's final two annual messages were therefore written communications. The only reference to his illness was made in 1919 when the President wrote: "I sincerely regret that I cannot be present at the opening of this session of the Congress. I am thus prevented from presenting in as direct a way as I could wish the many questions that are pressing for solution at this time."[20]

The emphasis on surveying domestic problems persisted. Despite the opportunity now presented by the written form for more detailed argumentation and factual reporting, Wilson retained his customary format and his 1920 message was second in brevity to his legislative mandate of 1916. In contrast to the buoyant, confident, compelling leadership expressed in his first five annual messages, the post-war Wilson reports reflected his loss of prestige and influence. The concluding sentences in 1920 acknowledged that "I do not feel it to be my privilege at present to suggest the detailed and particular methods" by which his recommendations should be carried out. "I have not so much laid before you a series of recommendations," he said, "as sought to utter a confession of faith, of the faith in which I was bred and which it is my solemn purpose to stand by until my last fighting days."

The subject matter content of the Wilson messages turned out to be very different from what the President thought it would be when, like Jefferson, he hopefully outlined a program of domestic reform in his first inaugural address. He set the tone for the "era of the New Freedom" when he declared, "Our duty is to cleanse, to reconsider, to restore, to correct the evil without impairing the good, to purify and humanize every process of our common life without weakening or sentimentalizing it." His chief concern was with domestic matters; foreign affairs were all but neglected. Similarly, his first annual message was devoted entirely to domestic issues except for a one paragraph reference to the Bryan "cooling-off" treaties, and strife-torn Mexico where the President felt confident that constitutional government would triumph and the United States would not have to alter its policy of "watchful waiting." Wilson was also sanguine about the "growing cordiality and sense of community of interest among the nations, foreshadowing an age of settled peace and good will." This was in 1913; Presidents do not necessarily make good oracles.

Wilson's 1913 and 1914 messages carried many recommendations for domestic reform: revision of the banking and currency system, rural credit extension, increase in power for the Bureau of Mines, enactment of an employer's liability law to assist railroad workers, assistance to the merchant marine, and support for a system of primary elections to select presidential nominees. "Outside of the charmed circle of our own national life," the scholar-President was insisting that we act as "trustees" of Puerto Rico, Hawaii, and the Philippines, holding "steadily in view the ultimate independence" of the latter.

With World War I underway in Europe, Wilson's cares multiplied. In December, 1914, he argued that it had always been clear and settled United States policy to oppose a large standing army. Determined though it was to defend itself, America would not be turned into a "military camp." We would not "ask our young men to spend the best years of their lives making soldiers of themselves." Wilson said that development and strengthening of the National Guard would be consistent with national traditions and a prudent provision for peace and safety, but more than this "would mean merely that we had lost our self-possession, that we had been thrown off our balance by a war with which we had nothing to do, whose causes can not touch us, whose very existence affords us opportunities of friendship and disinterested service which should make us ashamed of any thought of hostility or fearful preparation for trouble."[21]

The President reversed his position after the sinking of the *Lusitania*. By December 1915 he strongly advocated a comprehensive program of national defense. His change of heart was based on the recognition of hard facts: "Since I last had the privilege of addressing you on the state of the Union the war of nations on the other side of the sea, which had then only begun to disclose its portentious proportions, has extended its threatening and sinister scope until it has swept within its flame some portion of every quarter of the globe, not excepting our own hemisphere, has altered the whole face of international affairs, and now presents a prospect of reorganization and reconstruction such as statesmen and peoples have never been called upon to attempt before."[22]

Congress was urged to strengthen the army and navy and provide for the enlistment of 400,000 men . The Monroe Doctrine was stated as an American policy of non-interference in the domestc affairs of Latin-American republics.   Strict neutrality toward the warring nations was demanded. "The single thought of this message," Wilson said, "is national efficiency and security."

In 1916, his influence enhanced by re-election, Wilson restricted his report to a call for further enactment of unfinished phases of his domestc program.   His administration had already provided the leadership for more important legislation than any since Lincoln; but he didn't intend to let the threat of war cut that record short. Among the recommendations were: an eight-hour day for railway workers employed in interstate commerce, the emergency control of portions of the railroads in case of military necessity, the promotion of vocational and industrial education by federal aid, and assistance in perfecting the efficiency of the Interstate Commerce Commission.

When war came to the United States Wilson spoke out in conscious awareness that he now had a world audience. His address of 1917 insisted that "We shall regard the war as won only when the German people say to us, through properly accredited representatives, that they are ready to agree to a settlement based upon justice and reparation of the wrongs their rulers have done."   The President pledged that the war should not end in "vindictive action of any kind"; no nation or people were to be "robbed or punished because the irresponsible rulers of a single country have themselves done deep and abominable wrong."   Wilson stressed: "No annexations, no contributions, no punitive indemnities."

One year later the war was over and Wilson, in the tradition of the wartime Presidents, paid glowing tribute to the fighters on the military and home fronts: "Those of us who stayed home did our duty; . . . but for many a long day we shall think ourselves 'accurs'd we were not there, and hold our manhoods cheap while any speaks that fought'. . . .   The memory of those days of triumphant battle will go with these fortunate men to their graves; and each will have his favorite memory." He characterized the approaching peace talks in Paris as "of transcendent importance both to us and to the rest of the world." He knew of "no business or interest which should take precedence of them."

Still, there were other matters demanding attention. The message of 1918 and the ones which followed were devoted primarily to domestic rather than foreign affairs. The President saw "The problem of our return to peace [as] a problem of economic and industrial readjustment." His recommendations included: support for a program of public works, woman suffrage, continuation of the navy building program, construction of a series of reclamation projects, reduction in taxes, institution of a Budget Bureau, a lower tariff ("If we want to sell, we must be prepared to buy," he said), land grants for veterans, and stringent economies in government spending.

The outbreak of violence between labor and capital in the postwar period brought forth some professorial lectures from Wilson. He argued that "Labor must not be longer treated as a commodity," and he saw the role of government as the protector of "the rights of men collectively to bargain" for their legitimate objectives. He also believed that "capital should receive a reasonable return upon its investments" and that it was "entitled to protection at the hands of the Government in every emergency." He took note of the "widespread conditions of political restlessness" but was confident that the causes were superficial rather than deep-seated and would rapidly disappear with the return to normal conditions. He cautioned Congress not to be impatient or drastic in dealing with the problem but to seek the removal of the conditions upon which dissatisfaction bred. This particular annual message of 1919 concluded with the warning that "Russia today, with its blood and terror, is a painful object lesson of the power of minorities" and an example to those who would "take the shorter road of disorder and revolution." In America, Wilson said, "the instrument of all reform is the ballot" and those who propose "any other method of reform are enemies of this country."

Warren G. Harding left little doubt as to his position before or after his election: "The President would announce his program, which the Constitution directed him to do, but after that, legislation would be the work of Congress."[28] In his first "state of the union" report he hastened to assure his former Congressional colleagues that "we shall have no conflict of opinion about constitutional duties or authority." He charged that necessity born of war demands had led to "excessive grants of authority and an extra-ordinary concentration of powers in the chief executive." These powers would be restored to Congress with the repeal and expiration of wartime legislation, Harding said, and he further assured his audience: "Encroachment upon the functions of Congress or attempted dictation of its policy are not to be thought of, much less attempted, but there is an insistent call for harmony of purpose and concord of action to speed the solution of difficult problems confronting both the legislative and executive branches of the Government."[24]

His two annual addresses produced a definite return to the pre-Wilson type despite the fact that Harding continued the in person delivery. About 6,000 words each in length, the reports dealt with a multitude of subjects; little attempt was made to break the surface and examine the roots of the issues. Harding blandly performed his annual chore, content to leave the responsibility for legislation wholly with Congress. His 1922 message after having adverted to a variety of subjects contained this clue to Harding's sense of duty: "We are so vast and so varied in our national interests that scores of problems are pressing for attention. I must not risk the wearying of your patience with detailed references." The address then skipped along, touching only lightly on many more items. Harding fulfilled his duty "to report and recommend" without "wearying" the patience of the audience in this way: "Reclamation and irrigation projects, where waste land may be made available for settlement and productivity, are worthy of your favorable consideration." As for the fuel problem it was now under study "by a very capable fact-finding commission, and any attempt to deal with the coal problem, of such deep concern to the entire nation, must await the report of the Commision."

Disinclined to lead—indeed, probably incapable of leading—Harding re-established the trend toward the profuse, survey-type message which lost its way in a maze of topics arbitrarily lumped together and labeled "state of the union." Its oral form alone prevented a return to the extended messages which had been resisted by but a few of the Presidents. Subject areas in the Harding messages included: veteran benefits, the tariff, labor-capital disputes, the "recrudescence of hyphenated Americanism," immigration legislation, child labor abolition, conservation projects—to mention a few. Emphasis was on the domestic scene in keeping with the President's assurance in 1921 that "It is not my purpose to bring you a program of world restoration." The announcement that "the first budget is before you" initiated the practice of having the Budget Message submitted along with the annual message in the first days of the regular congressional session.

Hope was high in 1921 that world wars were a thing of the past. Harding observed of the Washington Naval conference then in session that "A most gratifying world-accomplishment is not improbable." One year later he expressed confidence in the Four Power Pact which he felt "abolishes every probability of war in the Pacific, . . . and I can well believe it might be made a model for like assurances wherever in the world any common interests are concerned."

In one respect at least, Wilson's and Harding's messages presented a continuity—in humanitarian considerations. In 1918 Wilson had urged establishment of export priorities and supply for the benefit of the destitute peoples of Northern France and Belgium, and in 1920, he had advocated a loan "to the struggling government of Armenia." Harding in 1921 called attention of the American people to their "fellow human beings who are suffering and dying of starvation in Russia." He made an ardent plea for assistance to "a people blameless and helpless in famine's peril" and recommended an appropriation of "10,000,000 bushels of corn and 1,000,000 bushels of seed grains." The fact that "we do not recognize the government of Russia, nor tolerate the propaganda which emanates therefrom" should not, Harding argued, "prevent us from putting aside fundamental differences in government when suffering and dying is going on."

Came Vice President Calvin Coolidge to the presidency in 1923. If anything, he was even less concerned than had been Harding about exercising the kind of presidential leadership which had been nourished so conscientiously by Theodore Roosevelt and Wilson. He accepted as President and party leader the responsibility to do the best he could to translate the platform into law but said in his *Autobiography*: "I have never felt that it was my duty to attempt to coerce Senators or Representatives, or to make reprisals. The people sent them to Washington. I felt I had discharged my duty when I had done the best I could with them. In this way I avoided almost entirely a personal opposition, which I think was of more value to the country than to attempt to prevail through arousing personal fear."[25]

Coolidge brought to the message the same spirit that he showed in all things: he was cautious, conservative, prudent, thorough, and unimaginative. No desire to lead a crusade for a better world motivated him. His 1926 message set forth his creed squarely: "What the country requires is not so much new policies as a steady

continuation of those which are already being crowned with such
abundant success." From his oral first "state of the union" address
in 1923 to his final one in 1928—written, like all the others after
the first one—Coolidge followed an almost identical pattern of
reporting. The messages, one of which made reference to as many
as forty subjects, were divided under topical headings. His reputation for taciturnity was not sustained; almost all of his annual messages exceeded in length those of Wilson and Harding. His longest,
in 1925, was over 13,000 words. By 1928 an old criticism was
being voiced: "Common misfortune of the Presidential Annual
Message is that they tend to become a catch-all. Being that they
often catch nothing."[26]

In 1923 Coolidge stated his position on world affairs succinctly:
"Our country has definitely refused to adopt and ratify the covenant
of the League of Nations. We have not felt warranted in assuming
the responsibilities which its members have assumed. I am not
proposing any change in this policy; neither is the Senate. The
incident, so far as we are concerned, is closed. The League exists
as a foreign agency. We hope it will be helpful. But the United
States sees no reason to limit its own freedom and independence of
action by joining it. We shall do well to recognize this basic fact
in all national affairs and govern ourselves accordingly." [27]

The rest of the report was an outspoken commentary on the
leading issues of the day, providing a view in miniature of his
unchanging position throughout most of his two terms: support of
membership in the World Court, opposition to the cancellation of
the war debts, advocacy of tax reductions, demand for prohibition
enforcement, encouragement of government aid to business and
commerce, and insistance that the tariff law should not be constantly revised. Warnings against extravagance in government and
the evil of federal paternalism provided the mortar for the brick-like
topical construction of the Coolidge annual messages.

A rare admission of recommendations coming directly from neither
President nor Congress was made in 1923: "The American Legion
will present to Congress a legislative program too extensive for
detailed discussion here. . . . While some of it I do not favor,
with much of it I am in hearty accord, and I recommend that a
most painstaking effort be made to provide remedies for any defects
in the administration of the present laws which their experience
has revealed. The attitude of the Government toward these pro-

posals should be one of generosity. But I do not favor the granting of a bonus."[28]

The election of Herbert Hoover in 1928 did nothing to change the standing of Congress as the pre-eminent branch of the federal government. His respect for the doctrine of legislative supremacy and his aversion to the exercise of presidential leadership posed no threat to the power position of the lawmakers. The initiation and formulation of legislation was the province of Congress; the President reserved for himself the duty of recommending the area in which the legislation was needed. C. Perry Patterson says that "Hoover accepted the Whig-Republican doctrine that a strong executive who championed the cause of the masses was dangerous to liberty. He thought that the safety of society lay in legislative bodies rather than in the hands of ambitious executives."[29]

By annual message time in December, 1929, the President had the unenviable duty of making reference to a "state of the union" already too painfully known to Congress and the public. Like Coolidge, Hoover preferred the written message, headings, and the well-organized, balanced survey. Commenting on his first message, the *New York Times* observed editorially: "Hoover is not able to escape the custom which prescribes that messages should be too long and too miscellaneous to be read generally."[30]

Gradually the pressure of deteriorating economic conditions pushed foreign affairs references toward practical exclusion until, in 1931, Hoover reverted to a practice introduced by Taft; he sent a special report on foreign relations two days after the annual message. His final document, still clinging to the use of headings with its continued emphasis on factual reporting, clearly reflected the overriding national interest in economic matters. All references to non-economic questions were grouped together in one single paragraph, headed: "Other Legislation." A foreign affairs section was omitted and the President begged off from further summarization, though the message, scarcely 4,000 words in length, was for him unusually brief; he relied upon the fact that "every detail of the Government is covered in the reports to Congress" giving information about the regular and emergency activities of which, "even the briefest review . . . would render the annual message unduly long." The *New York Times* commended this report for having the "merit of being short and clear" and went on to observe that the

President was tired and discouraged and the financial situation "not exactly exhilarating."[31]

Old subject entries were joined by new ones in the Hoover annual reports. Perennials such as the tariff, merchant marine, civil service, immigration, and conservation were joined by newcomers sired by technological development: highway construction, commercial aviation control, electric power regulation, radio transmission allotment, and Muscle Shoals disposition. Prohibition was a transient issue of the 1920s; Indian doings, for the first time, failed to get any notice.

In foreign affairs, Hoover reported on the progress of the Kellogg-Briand Pact, urged U.S. membership in the World Court, reminded Congress that "We still have marines on foreign soil—in Nicaragua, Haiti, and China," hailed the signing of the London Naval Pact as having "abolished competition in the building of warships," advised Congress that German reparations and other inter-government debts had been postponed for one year, and was apprehensive over the "difficulties between China and Japan."

Regarding the general world situation Hoover observed in 1931: "Within two years there have been revolutions or acute social disorders in 19 countries, embracing more than half the population of the world. Ten countries have been unable to meet their external obligations. In 14 countries, embracing a quarter of the world's population, former monetary standards have been temporarily abandoned. In a number of countries there have been acute financial panics or compulsory restraints upon banking. These disturbances have many roots in the dislocations from the World War. Every one of them has reacted upon us."[32]

A heavy emphasis on economic conditions quite naturally distinguished the text of the Hoover messages. The 1929 report did achieve a balanced view of the "state of the union," but the next two devoted over half their content to questions arising from the Great Depression, and the final one was almost exclusively concerned with them. His 1931 message significantly even included a section starkly labeled "Unemployment." Hoover concluded this portion of the report by reiterating his position on the role which government should play: "I am opposed to any direct or indirect Government dole. The breakdown and increased unemployment in Europe is due in part to such practices. Our people are providing against distress from unemployment in true American fashion by a magnificent response to public appeal and by action of the local governments."[33]

This philosophy of reliance on local and individual responsibility plus the belief that recovery could be hastened by government loans to private industries was illustrated over and over in Hoover's annual messages.   The final words of his 1932 report constituted a swan song of Rugged Individualism: "On the social and economic sides, the background of our American system and the motivation of progress is essentially that we should allow free play of social and economic forces as far as will not limit equality of opportunity and as will at the same time stimulate the initiative and enterprise of our people.   In the maintenance of this balance the Federal Government can permit of no privilege to any person or any group.   It should act as a regulatory agent and not as a participant in economic and social life.   The moment the Government participates, it becomes a competitor with the people.   As a competitor it becomes at once a tyranny in whatever direction it may touch."[34]

By 1932 the in person "state of the union" message seemed doomed to disuse and the survey-type report appeared to have regained acceptance.   This was not surprising in one sense; the Presidents in the 1920s did not consider themselves either as prime ministers or prime movers.   Harold Laski characterized the period as an "era of conscious abdication from power on the part of the president."[35] At the same time that the Republican Presidents were shying away from leadership, technological development in mass communication was increasing the effectiveness with which a forceful President could influence public opinion.   In 1917, a news article under the headline "Whole World Gets Wilson Message" reported that, "President Wilson's address to Congress was heralded . . . throughout the world by the United States Government.   Nearly every known means of communication—express train, telephone, telegraph, wireless, and submarine cable—was utilized in transmitting the message."[36]

And by December 6, 1923, radio was available to the President. The *New York Times* reported:

"The voice of President Coolidge, addressing Congress . . . will be carried over a greater portion of the United States and will be heard by more people than the voice of any man in history.

"Arrangements were completed . . . for broadcasting the President's address as delivered in the chamber of the House of Representatives through six powerful radio stations and it is expected by the engineers in charge that fully a million persons will hear Mr. Coolidge speak."[37]

On the following day the *Times* informed its readers "there was no discoverable instance of a person equipped with a receiving set

who did not use it to listen to Coolidge's address." Many social
affairs with friends invited to come and listen to the President were
reported. In downtown New York City, hundreds of radio apparatus
stores broadcast the address through loud speakers to knots of listeners
"drawn together to listen intently to the words of their President,
not as embalmed text, but as living things while he was in the very
act of speaking them."[38] Coolidge, however, was apparently unim-
pressed. One year later, he gave up the opportunities offered by
radio and submitted a written message; a practice which was then
followed to the end of Hoover's administration. Public-spirited
citizens of the 1920s complained that the American people were
losing interest in politics. But the style of Harding and the personality
of Coolidge and Hoover were poorly suited to command the serious
notice of a population, at first prosperous and complacent and later
depression-ridden and disillusioned.

Harding was able to conjure up a plentiful flow of verbiage at
short notice and he enjoyed speaking, or as he himself phrased it,
"to bloviate." Ambiguity was often accompanied by triteness—as,
for example, in the 1922 Harding figure of speech: "It would be
folly to ignore that we live in a motor age. The motor car reflects
our standard of living and guages the speed of our present-day life.
It long ago ran down Simple Living, and never halted to inquire
about the prostrate figure which fell as its victim."

In a contrast as marked as the differences in their personality,
Coolidge's style with its emphasis on terseness and simplicity compared favorably to the sonorous rhetoric of Harding. In a rare excursion into the realm of "lecturing," Coolidge would swiftly and
logically make his point: "It would appear to be elementary that
the more the Government expends the more it must require every
producer to contribute out of his production to the Public Treasury,
and the less he will have for his own benefit. The continuing costs
of public administration can be met in only one way—by the work
of the people. The higher they become, the more the people must
work for the Government. The less they are, the more the people
can work for themselves."[39]

Hoover continued in the Coolidge manner of methodical, systematic, colorless, and concise message composition. Occasionally, he
allowed himself to make use of expressions borrowed from engineer-
ing experience, as in 1931: "We must put some steel beams in the
foundation of our credit structure." One year later, he assessed
the function of the banking and financial system to be "in furnishing

the essential lubricant to the wheels of industry, agriculture, and commerce, that is, credit." The *New York Times* summed up the impact of Hoover's annual reports when in referring to one of them, it commented: "One rises from reading the President's message to Congress yesterday with the feeling that it is in general correct but cold."[40]

With Wilson the results had been infinitely better even without the advantage that radio would have added to his command of public attention. Probably without equal among his contemporaries as an effective speaker, he was able to combine an almost poetic simplicity and soaring eloquence with a moral earnestness that impressed his listeners as well as his readers.[41] He needed this talent to dramatize the far reaching changes which he sought to make. Similarly, realistic reporting came more naturally and more readily from the reformer Wilson than from the standpat chief executives of the 1920s. A gradual if uneven tendency to admit difficulties in the state of the union began to show up also when the Presidents were unable to ignore "reality" at the expense of casting doubt on the validity of their messages in general.

In 1913 Wilson brashly charged that because of "backwardness and neglect on our part," the lack of adequate farm credit in the United States was a "handicap and embarrassment" which might be corrected by a study of European rural credit systems. His statement of needed reform usually preceded his suggested solution; the logical progression employed by champion debaters—and professors. A typical example of this technique is Wilson's "lecture" of 1914: "Governments grow, piecemeal, both in their tasks and in the means by which those tasks are to be performed, and very few Governments are organized, I venture to say, as wise and experienced businessmen would organize them if they had a clean sheet of paper to write upon. Certainly the Government of the United States is not. I think it is generally agreed that there should be a systematic reorganization and reassembling of its parts so as to secure greater efficiency and effect considerable savings in expense."[42]

Harding, suprisingly perhaps, was more realistic in publicly recognizing national reverses than had been many of his more zealous and dedicated predecessors. The fact of an "actual depression in our agricultural industry" was admitted in 1921, and his reference to the eighteenth amendment was blunt and honest: "In plain speaking, there are conditions relating to its enforcement which savor of nation-wide scandal. It is the most demoralizing factor in public life." Still, the temptation to extol the unique virtue of the American economy could not be resisted and Harding did a little boasting about it in 1922: "Surely we have been fortunate in diminishing unemployment, and our industrial and business activities, which are the lifeblood of our material existence, have beer restored as in no other reconstruction period of like length in th history of the world."

With Coolidge in the White House, the upward swing of optimism reached its zenith. In 1924 he disclaimed the belief that America had no problems but he did insist that "Our country is almost unique in its ability to discharge fully and promptly all its obligations at home and abroad, and provide for all its inhabitants an increase in material resources, in intellectual vigor and in moral power. The nation holds a position unsurpassed in all former human experience."[43]

Two years later Coolidge chided the public for failing to appreciate how well off they were: "The American people are altogether lacking in an appreciation of the tremendous good fortune that surrounds their international position. We have no traditional enemies. We are not embarrassed over any disputed territory. We have no possessions that are coveted by others; they have none that are coveted by us. Our borders are unfortified. We fear none; no one fears us."[44]

The President's negative attitude toward sweeping legislative changes was in tune with the popular belief in the natural progress of material prosperity. As Will Rogers observed, "He didn't do anything, but that's what the people wanted done." The *New York Times* found consolation in the dull Coolidge annual messages: "The old saying might be revised to read that nation is happy when the Presidential messages are unexciting."[45]

In December, 1928, a "lame-duck" but very "bullish" Coolidge misread the handwriting on the wall when he cheerfully greeted the lawmakers with the gladdening forecast that, "No Congress of the United States ever assembled, on surveying the state of the union, has met with a more pleasing report than that which appears at present, . . . [and] the country can anticipate the future with optimism."

Although the consequences of the Wall Street market crash and the early manifestations of the Great Depression were starkly evident when Hoover presented his first annual report, his assessment of the "state of the union" was little affected thereby: " . . . I wish to emphasize that during the past year the Nation has continued to grow in strength; our people have advanced in comfort; we have gained in knowledge, the education of youth has been more widely spread; moral and spiritual forces have been maintained; peace has become more assured. The problems with which we are confronted are the problems of growth and of progress." [46]

He did warn against the "unwarranted pessimism and fear" generated by the sudden threat of unemployment and the recollection of the consequences of previous crashes; but, in his opinion, the growth of organized crime and the increase in the volume of crimes of all kinds constituted "the most serious issue before our people."

The economic crisis went on deepening but no corresponding depression gripped the annual message. In 1930 Hoover advised Congress and the public that "the fundamental strength of the Nation's economic life is unimpaired; . . . " He asserted that the major forces of the depression lay outside the United States and many factors gave encouragement for the future. "We should remember," he said, "that these conditions have been met many times before, that they are but temporary, that our country is today stronger and richer in resources, in equipment, in skill, than ever in its history. We are in an extraordinary degree self-sustaining, we will overcome world influences and will lead the march of prosperity as we have always done hitherto." [47]

A year later the President faced up somewhat more manfully to the facts: "The chief influence affecting the state of the Union during the past year has been the continued world-wide economic disturbances", but he went on to suggest philosophically that even amid the depression, fundamental gains had been made: "Business depressions have been recurrent in the life of our country and are but transitory. The Nation has emerged from each of them with increased strength and virility because of the enlightenment they have brought, the readjustment and the larger understanding of the realities and obligations of life and work which come from them." [48]

The President persisted in blaming the absence of economic recovery on the "unjustified lack of confidence," insisting that "Our first step toward recovery is to reestablish confidence and thus restore the flow of credit which is the very basis of our economic life." The facts of the situation were too painfully obvious to allow a wholesale disregard for the real "state of the union" and Hoover's reports, accordingly, did contain many references to the difficulties and hardships of the period. The over-all tone and spirit, however, were always those of reassurance and trust in the recuperative powers of the American system. Hoover never let a pessimistic note ring out in his annual messages without a compensating optimistic echo. In sharp contrast is the appraisal he made on August 11, 1932, in accepting re-nomination at the Republican convention: "The past three years have been a time of unparalleled economic calamity. They have been years of greater suffering and hardship than any which have come to the American people since the aftermath of the Civil War."

In December of the same year the President's "state of the union" message told of his satisfaction with the advances in the areas of peace, national defense, education and science, public health, and the "far larger degree of freedom from industrial conflict then hitherto known." Hoover commended the "magnificent sense of humanity" demonstrated daily by the people in spite of the widespread hardships and he saw this "individual and community responsibility" as evidence that "They [the people] have grown in their conceptions and organization for cooperative action for the common welfare."

Later in the message, referring to the failure of the financial system, Hoover did report that "The losses, suffering, and tragedies of our people are incalculable . . . millions of . . . people have suffered in the loss of their homes and farms, . . . unemployment increased, and farmer's prices diminished." But in his evaluation of the general economic situation Hoover again saw the "turn toward recovery" having been reached, and the credit for this "improvement of conditions in many parts of the country" was assigned to the "unprecedented emergency measures enacted and policies adopted which undoubtedly saved the country from economic disaster."

The true state of the union, however, did not match Hoover's assessment. His understandable attempt to encourage confidence by speaking bravely did not, in the end, bring about recovery. Apparently one could not talk one's way out of a depression.

The post-Civil War trend of minimizing or excluding completely religious thanksgiving in the annual messages continued. Harding and Hoover made none at all; Coolidge, when he did include such sentiments, did so in a simple expression of accommodation to the "Divine Will."[49] Wilson had been similarly sparing in making religious mention. He made only passing reference to "God's providence" in 1914; but his message in 1917, coming eight months after the U.S. entry into World War I, concluded with a reference to "the hand of God"; and one year later, saluting the war victory, he expressed the nation's thanks to God. His 1917 "state of the union" message provides an illustration of Ralph H. Gabriel's contention that the rationalization for American participation in World War I "took unconsciously the form of a morality play. It was the story of a hero provoked by a villain to mortal combat."[50] Less than one year after his "Peace Without Victory" plea Wilson called for the "vigorous, rapid and successful promotion of the great task of winning the war" on the grounds that:

"We can do this with all the greater zeal and enthusiasm because we know that for us this is a war of high principle, debased by no selfish ambitions of conquest or spoilation; . . . The purpose of the Central Powers strikes straight at the very heart of everything we believe in; their methods of warfare outrage every principle of humanity and of knightly honor. . . .

"It is because it is for us a war of high, disinterested purpose, . . . that we feel ourselves doubly constrained to propose for its outcome only that which is righteous and of irreproachable intention, . . . The cause being just and holy, the settlement must be of like motive and equality. For this we can fight, but for nothing less noble or less worthy of our traditions."[51]

The annual message continued to omit any mention of presidential elections thus maintaining an institutional continuity of its own. There were no references to the change in administrations, no farewells, no recognition of political parties. An unusual warmth and conciliatory attitude toward Congress was evinced generally; and Wilson, until 1919, consistently included expressions of good will toward the legislators. The concluding paragraph of his first address made an unique interpretation: "Surely it is a proper and pertinent part of my report on 'the state of the union' to express my admiration for the diligence, the good temper, and the full comprehension of public duty which has already been manifested by both the Houses."

In December, 1918, Wilson was preparing for the peace negotiations which were to be held in Paris a month later; he politely and deferentially asked the hostile, Republican controlled Congress for co-operation: "May I not hope, . . . that in the delicate tasks I shall have to perform . . . I may have the encouragement and added strength of your combined support? . . . I shall count on your friendly countenance and encouragement. . . . I shall make my trip as brief as possible. . . ."

The following year his illness created a technical problem for the lawmakers. The customary practice had been for each House to appoint a committee to call on the President and notify him that Congress was organized and ready to receive his message. In 1919, however, Wilson was too ill to receive them. The committees accomplished their mission by written notes rather than personal visits and the dilemma was resolved.[52] On December 2nd Wilson's seventh annual message was transmitted to the Capitol where it was read by the clerks in both Houses and the sequence of yearly reports, dating back to 1790, continued unbroken.

Chapter Seven

THE PRESIDENT VIEWS THE WORLD

The year was 1933. Franklin D. Roosevelt expressed the hope in his first inaugural address that "the normal balance of executive and legislative authority may be wholly adequate to meet the unprecedented task before us." He warned, however, that should Congress fail to act promptly on his recommended emergency measures "I shall not evade the clear course of duty that will confront me. I shall ask the Congress for the one remaining instrument to meet the crisis—broad executive power to wage a war against emergency, as great as the power that would be given to me if we were in fact invaded by a foreign foe. For the trust reposed in me I will return the courage and the devotion that befit the times. I can do no less."[1]

It had been three and one half years since the beginning of the Great Depression—"the greatest debacle known in the financial history of the United States and the world"[2]—and the President spoke at a time of national despair unparalleled in American history except for the Civil War period. A special session of Congress convened five days after his inaugural and began its historic one hundred days of lawmaking which produced an unprecedented amount of legislation. With energy and skill strongly reminiscent of Wilson's, Roosevelt succeeded even better than his Democratic predecessor in managing Congress as though it were his parliament and he its prime minister. He saw the presidency not only as the nation's highest office but also as a "place of moral leadership." All the "great Presidents," Roosevelt said, "had been leaders of thought at critical times in the nation's history.[3] James MacGregor Burns characterizes F.D.R. during 1933-34 as neither a Jefferson nor a Jackson; to him it seemed that Roosevelt provided "broker leadership" dealing with and mediating among the leaders of organized groups, farmers, and businessmen.[4]

While governor of New York, F.D.R. had been required by the state constitution to report to the legislature "on the state of his office." His messages had been broadly drawn to include the public in his audience as well. He carried a similar interpretation to the national capital stating on March 11, 1933: "The Constitution has

101

laid upon me the duty of conveying the condition of the country to Congress assembled at Washington. I believe that I have a like duty to convey to the people themselves a clear picture of the situation at Washington itself whenever there is danger of any confusion as to what the government is undertaking."[5]

The twentieth amendment moved up the convening date of Congress from the first week in December to the first week in January. It became effective in October of 1933, thereby eliminating the annual message of that year. On January 3, 1934, Roosevelt appeared before Congress to deliver his "state of the union" address—the first President to do so since 1923. F.D.R. favored the Wilsonian pattern: a finely knit, unified speech with its attendant attention-demanding ceremonial replaced the kaleidoscopic, clerk-read messages of Coolidge and Hoover. Taking advantage of radio, the annual address more than ever before was directed at a national and world audience rather than merely to Congress. Factual reporting was kept to a minimum and was included not so much for the information of the lawmakers but for its use as a launching base for specific presidential recommendations, policy proposals, and general observations.

Roosevelt's first annual address took only twenty-two minutes and because of its almost total lack of recommendations was not a typical one for him. His purpose was revealed in his opening remarks: "I come before you at the opening of the regular session of the 73rd Congress, not to make requests for special or detailed items of legislation; I come, rather, to counsel with you, who, like myself, have been selected to carry out a mandate of the whole people, . . ."[6]

In a message devoid of detailed facts and figures, F.D.R. briefly sketched a progress report on domestic and foreign affairs with emphasis on the former, and indicated the general areas which he felt needed further attention. He was understandably pleased with the "fine relationship" which had brought so many administration favored bills to his desk for signature: "Out of these friendly contacts we are, fortunately, building a strong and permanent tie between the legislative and executive branches of the Government. The letter of the Constitution wisely declared a separation, but the impulse of common purpose declares a Union. In this spirit we join once more in serving the American people."[7]

A year later Roosevelt shifted the emphasis from general reporting to specific recommendations. This time he used the message to announce the "Second New Deal":

"In defining immediate factors which enter into our quest, I have spoken to the Congress and the people of three great divisions:

1. The security of a livelihood through the better use of the national resources of the land in which we live.
2. The security against the major hazards and vicissitudes of life.
3. The security of decent homes.

"I am now ready to submit to Congress a broad program designed ultimately to establish all three of these factors of security—a program which because of the many lost years will take many future years to fulfill."[8]

That Roosevelt never considered the yearly report as being intended for Congress alone is clearly shown by a remark in his first "fireside chat" of 1935: "Since my annual message to the Congress on January 4th, I have not addressed the general public over the air."[9] The next year, Congress convened in the evening to receive the President's "state of the union" message—the only time that it has not been given in the afternoon. This unusual circumstance provided F.D.R. with a nation wide radio audience at the prime hour of nine p.m. and immediately drew criticism from Republicans who demanded equal radio time to answer the President's speech on the grounds that the congressional decision to meet at night had been politically inspired by the upcoming 1936 national election.[10] To a large extent the Republicans were right. Roosevelt did use the occasion to make a spirited defense of his party's legislative record and to challenge his opponents to "no longer hide their dissent in a cowardly cloak of generality. Let them define the issue. We have been specific in our affirmative action. Let them be specific in their negative attack." A reference near the end of the speech to "this message on the state of the union" drew great bursts of derisive laughter, according to a *New York Times* reporter, from the Republican side of the House.[11]

On January 6, 1937, Roosevelt pointed out that because of the twentieth amendment which moved the inauguration day of the chief executive from March fourth to January twentieth, "For the first time in our history a President delivers his annual message to a new Congress within a fortnight of the expiration of his term of office. While there is no change in the presidency this year, change will occur in future years." It is interesting to note that he did not say that change would occur in four years—which would have been true if Roosevelt limited himself to the traditional two terms. "It is my belief," he added "that under the new constitutional practice, the President should in every fourth year, in so far as seems reasonable, review the existing state of our national affairs and outline broad future problems, leaving specific recommendations for future legislation to be made by the President about to be inaugurated."[12]

Since, however, the proffered advice did not apply to his current situation, F.D.R. proceeded to delineate a detailed plan for immediate congressional action. As long as Congress recognized the need for leadership and acknowledged its inability to provide the necessary initiative, the President's lead was not seriously challenged. With a lessening of pressure for new legislation, however, the rule that "congressional docility speedily evaporates" was illustrated. By his second term, despite his re-election with almost unanimous approval of the electoral college, Roosevelt's influence with Congress was on the decline and never recovered the full bloom of the 1933 "honeymoon days."

"The storm signals from across the sea" of which Roosevelt warned gradually crowded references to domestic matters from the annual messages of 1938, 1939 and 1940.[13] With prophetic directness, the President told Congress in 1941: "I address you, . . . at a moment unprecedented in the history of the Union. I use the word 'unprecedented' because at no previous time has American security been as seriously threatened from without as it is today." By January of the next year, the United States was at war with the Axis powers and F.D.R. used the message to report on the war's progress, to explain the strategic problems involved in fighting a global campaign, to state the objectives for which the struggle was being waged, to announce new and more ambitious production figures, and to boost morale with the assurance that, "The militarists of Berlin and Tokyo started this war. But the massed, angered forces of common humanity will finish it."

In 1943 Roosevelt devoted over half of the report to a review of the war effort: the *New York Times* called the message, "able, concise, well-balanced, and in some details, highly informative."[14] The trend toward the omission of recommendations and requests for specific legislation was continued but the President gave warning that it was time to start thinking about post-war adjustments. His observations while general were typical of his determined use of the annual message to keep the broad outlines of his proposed policies before both Congress and the American public.

Too ill to appear before Congress in 1944, F.D.R. nevertheless wanted his message to receive its usual attention. His solution was to deliver substantially the same address over the radio nine hours after it had been delivered to Congress in writing. His introductory radio remarks explained: "Only a few of the newspapers of the United States can print the message in full, and I am very anxious that the American people be given the opportunity to hear what I have recommended to Congress for this fateful year in our history— and the reasons for those recommendations."[15]

The report laid out a detailed legislative program with emphasis on domestic issues. In 1945 the President was again recovering from the "flu" and was not permitted to leave the White House; he sent a written message to Congress at noon and followed it in the evening with a radio address which repeated some parts of the congressional document. The message, freed from the restraint imposed by oral delivery, ran over 8,000 words, more than twice as long as most F.D.R. yearly reports. In response to a question at his press conference the previous day regarding the amount of space that the newspapers should reserve for reprinting the message, F.D.R. had replied: "Around eight thousand. Terrible. I am ashamed of it. But it's wartime. Wartime produces things out of proportion."[16] He justified as appropriate the comprehensive survey which reviewed, in his words, "the basic strategy which has guided us through three years of war, and which will lead, eventually, to total victory." The message also told of supply and manpower shortages, made suggestions for postwar planning, and included a short epilogue in which the President counseled unity and harmony between the three branches of the federal government.

Roosevelt remade the presidency in the twentieth century as Jackson had one hundred years earlier, raising it to its highest point of independence, prestige and vigor. The news appeal of the White House was exploited. F.D.R.'s dramatic and dynamic use of radio and the press conference nourished the tendency of the public to look to the chief executive as the source of national leadership. The annual report and special messages to Congress were skillfully employed to keep administration views and policies before the lawmakers and the people. Samuel Rosenman, longtime F.D.R. adviser, writes of Roosevelt's great confidence that "the mass of American people could understand long-range objectives just as thoroughly as immediate problems," and of his ability "to make them understood—better than any other President in our history. . . . "[17] Letters to the White House, 200 a week when Taft was President, now came at the rate of 5,000 per day—an indication of the popular response which was stimulated by F.D.R.[18]

Read by themselves the Roosevelt annual messages provide a succinct presidential "Short History of the United States and World Affairs from 1934 to 1945." The President's commentary though open to criticism and refutation as partisan, furnishes an unique White House version of the tumultuous years when the nation passed between the Scylla and Charybdis of depression and global war. The text of his "state of the union" reviews supports James M. Burns' contention that, compared to Roosevelt, "Probably no American politician has given so many speeches that were essentially sermons rather than statements of policy. Like a preacher, he wanted and expected his sermons to serve as practical guides to the people."[19]

In many ways, F.D.R.'s first annual address rang with echoes from twenty years before when, like Wilson, he devoted all but a few paragraphs to a consideration of domestic issues. He was determined, he said, to stop "the unnecessary expansion of industrial plants, the waste of natural resources, the exploitation of the consumers of natural monopolies, the accumulation of stagnant surpluses, child labor, and the ruthless exploitation of all labor, the encouragement of speculation with other people's money, ..."[20] In 1935 his audience was told that, "Throughout the world, change is the order of the day." The President's contribution was a call for a "new program of emergency public employment." The Works Progress Administration was subsequently created to carry out his declaration that, "The federal government must and shall quit this business of relief."

A year later F.D.R. was forced to turn his attention, momentarily at least, from his absorption in domestic reforms: "The temper and the purposes of the rulers of many of the great populations in Europe and in Asia have not pointed the way either to peace or to good-will among men. . . . A point has been reached where the people of the Americas must take cognizance of growing ill-will, of marked trends toward agression, of increasing armaments, of shortening tempers—a situation which has in it many of the elements that lead to the tragedy of general war."[21]

The picture presented was not completely new to his annual message audience. In 1934 F.D.R. had apologized for not being able to present "a picture of complete optimism" concerning world affairs, and in 1935, he had admitted, "I cannot with candor tell you that general international relationships outside the border of the United States are improved."

Roosevelt followed up his caveat of "autocracy in world affairs" with a condemnation of "autocratic institutions" within the United

States. Opponents of his administration were challenged to campaign on the issue of repealing New Deal measures. The election of 1936 resulted in a tremendous personal victory for the President and the return of Democratic majorities to both Houses. To the new Congress, he insisted the "vital need" was not "an alteration of our fundamental law, but an increasingly enlightened view with reference to it." The N.R.A. had been outlawed, he said, but the problems had not been outlawed and still remained. Means must be found "to adapt our legal forms and our judicial interpretations to the actual present national needs of the largest progressive democracy in the modern world." It was a stirring offensive in his battle against the Supreme Court that F.D.R. lost; the war he won, more or less.

By annual message time in 1938 Roosevelt had already delivered his "Quarantine Speech" in which he urged collective international co-operation against aggressors as the only means of preserving world peace. The criticism which it aroused within the country did not dissuade him from returning to the same theme in the opening remarks of his address to Congress. The bulk of the message, however, was an exhortation calling for a domestic legislative program which would implement his political philosophy: "Government has a final responsibility for the well-being of its citizenship. If private cooperative endeavor fails to provide work for willing hands and relief for the unfortunate, those suffering hardship from no fault of their own have a right to call upon the Government for aid; and a government worthy of its name must make fitting response."[22]

A tacit recognition that the flame of social reform was burning less brightly was indicated when the 1939 message recommended no new legislation. The President stressed the need for defense expenditures and warned of the threat posed to the United States by the gathering forces of aggression overseas: "Events abroad have made it increasingly clear to the American people that dangers within are less to be feared than dangers from without."

Again in 1940 foreign affairs dominated the message and only two recommendations for specific congressional approval were made: a demand for a heavily increased national defense program and a re-enactment of the expiring Reciprocal Trade Agreements Act.

The *New York Times* headlined its report of the President's 1941 address: "Roosevelt Asks All Out Aid to Democracies; Ships, Planes, Tanks, Guns."[23] F.D.R. called for a Lend-Lease program for the victims of the Axis powers and defied the dictators to place whatever

interpretation they wished on American actions. He warned that
the dictators would make war when they were ready:

"As long as the aggressor nations maintain the offensive, they—
not we—will choose the time and the place and the method of their
attack.

"That is why the future of all the American Republics is today
in serious danger. That is why this Annual Message to the Congress
is unique in our history."[24]

The President cautioned against diminishing concern about social
and economic amelioration. He unveiled the "Four Freedoms" as
a world foundation for the future.

The bombing of Pearl Harbor transformed the January, 1942 message into a wartime speech. Roosevelt, like Wilson, proclaimed to
the world the allied position: "Our own objectives are clear; the
objective of smashing the militarism imposed by war lords upon their
enslaved peoples—the objective of liberating the subjected Nations—
the objective of establishing and securing freedom of speech, freedom
of religion, freedom from want, and freedom from fear everywhere
in the world." [25] The war would end "as soon as we make it end, by
our combined efforts, our combined strength, our combined determination to fight through and work through until the end—the end of
militarism in Germany and Italy and Japan. Most certainly we shall
not settle for less."

Roosevelt set production figures for 1942 and 1943 with the second
year's goal to be 125,000 airplanes, 75,000 tanks, 35,000 anti-aircraft
guns, and 10,000,000 tons of shipping. Far from revealing military
secrets, F.D.R. hoped that the figures would "become common knowledge in Germany and Japan." The war news had been discouraging
and the time was still distant when military successes would be
reported but the President struck a militant note of confidence:

"We cannot wage this war in a defensive spirit. As our power
and our resources are fully mobilized, we shall carry the attack against
the enemy—we shall hit him and hit him again wherever and whenever we can reach him.

"We must keep him far from our shores, for we intend to bring this
battle to him on his own home grounds."[26]

The 1943 annual message was the first affirmatively optimistic
speech which Roosevelt allowed himself to deliver after Pearl Harbor.[27]
The military fronts were surveyed and a tribute paid to all the nations
which were fighting together against the Axis powers. New production goals were announced, home front efforts were praised, and

promise was held out for a better post-war world: "I do not prophesy when this war will end. But I do believe that this year of 1943 will give to the United Nations a very substantial advance along the roads that lead to Berlin and Rome and Tokyo. I tell you it is within the realm of possibility that this Seventy-eighth Congress may have the historic privilege of helping greatly to save the world from future fear."[28]

A year later the President was pushing a five-point legislative program which called for a "realistic tax law," continuation of war contract re-negotiations, a ceiling on food costs, re-enactment of the currency stabilization law, and a national service act which would prevent wartime strikes and make virtually every able-bodied adult available for essential service. He did not get what he wanted; the rebuke indicating that on domestic, civilian issues Roosevelt had lost control of both Congress and his own party. In the same message he continued to project generalized goals which the law-makers were urged to study and prepare to implement once the war was over. This time it was a "second Bill of Rights" by which the President would have Congress guarantee to all Americans, regardless of station, race, or creed:

"The right to a useful and remunerative job in the industries or shops or farms or mines of the Nation;

"The right to earn enough to provide adequate food and clothing and recreation;

"The right of every farmer to raise and sell his products at a return which will give him and his family a decent living;

"The right of every businessman, large and small, to trade in an atmosphere of freedom from unfair competition and domination by monopolies at home or abroad;

"The right of every family to a decent home;

"The right to adequate medical care and the opportunity to achieve and enjoy good health;

"The right to adequate protection from the economic fears of old age, sickness, accident, and unemployment;

"The right to a good education."[29]

The 1945 annual message was prepared as Roosevelt was making plans for the Yalta meeting. In it was reflected his anxiety about the capacity of the Allies to continue their wartime co-operation after the fighting stopped. The message reiterated his determination "to secure so far as is humanly possible the fulfillment of the principles of the Atlantic Charter." The President was sure of "ultimate victory" but he again pressed Congress to enact a national service law. He also called for the induction of nurses into the armed forces and for legislation to make the four million men classified as IV-F available in whatever capacity would benefit the war effort. Roosevelt reminded the lawmakers of their responsibility to plan for the sixty million jobs that would be needed, and he was of the opinion that universal military training after the war would be an "essential factor in the maintenance of peace in the future, . . . " The concluding paragraph of his final annual message looked forward to the end and beyond the war:

"Most important of all—1945 can and must see the substantial beginning of the organization of world peace. This organization must be the fulfillment of the promise for which men have fought and died in this war. It must be the justification of all the sacrifices that have been made—of all the dreadful misery that this world has endured. We Americans of today, together with our allies, are making history—and I hope it will be better history than ever has been made before.

"We pray that we may be worthy of the unlimited opportunities that God has given us."[30]

Roosevelt's death in 1945 thrust Harry S. Truman (whom a biographer characterized as "President in the Dark")[31] into the presidency. It was generally predicted that his administration would restore a more deferential and less demanding relationship between the executive and legislative branches. During his first year in office Truman fulfilled this expectation; the President stated his case and left legislative responsibility strictly to the lawmakers. In his initial appearance before Congress as President, four days after Roosevelt's death, and later in June to urge ratification of the United Nations Charter, he had been favorably received. His important post-war program was delivered in September, 1945 by written message and "his failure to appear in person might possibly have been another gesture of his recognition of the right of the legislative branch."[32] It was, therefore, not a complete surprise when Truman presented his first annual message in written form. Congress was convening at an unusually late date, January 14, 1946, having enjoyed an extended holiday vacation. The President had already delivered a radio address, entitled, "The state of the union," on January 3rd in which he said that "a regular report will be made soon after [Congress] reconvenes. Tonight I am speaking directly to you—the American people—on issues which will be the subject of debate when Congress returns."[83]

The White House originally planned to send the annual message to Congress on January 17th and have the Budget message follow on the 21st. Ever since the first separate Budget message, during the Harding administration, all the Presidents had presented these two documents serially soon after the legislators had assembled. On January 16th, however, Truman announced that the two reports would be combined in one: presidential Secretary Ross explained, "Two messages would mean a lot of overlapping. It's a wonder no one has thought of it before. As the President said, the budget is part of the state of the union."[84] The double duty document ran over 25,000 words. It was divided into three parts: I. From Peace to War; 11. The Federal Program; and III. The Budget for the Federal Program for the Fiscal Year of 1947.

The document's unusual length and its detailed treatment of both factual information and recommendations brought from the *New York Times* an editorial expressing doubt as to the effectiveness of lumping so much material into one communication: "The message reads less like a message than it does like a party platform, assembled from many ideas coming from many places, and it has all the characteristics of most party platforms, including a probable scarcity of readers. It is the very opposite of those pungent and forceful appeals with which Mr. Roosevelt used to spur Congress into action when he felt that a crisis was present or impending. Mr. Truman has not yet learned the art of shaping such a call to action. The lack of clear focus in his own message is one of the real handicaps in his present relations with Congress."[85]

Whereas excitement and overflow crowds had accompanied President Roosevelt's annual pilgrimages to the House chamber, half empty halls provided the audience for the frock-coated clerks who for more than two hours "delivered" Truman's message in unbroken monotonous tones. Most Congressmen remained in their offices.

Gradually, after 1946, Truman became less deferential to Congress and by 1948, bolstered by his surprise victory, became an open advocate of strong executive leadership. In his *Memoirs,* he wrote: "I believe that the power of the President should be used in the interest of the people, and in order to do that the President must use whatever power the Constitution does not expressly deny him." He saw himself bound to continue the work of the "strong liberal Presidents: Jefferson, Jackson, Lincoln, Theodore Roosevelt, Wilson,

Franklin Roosevelt."[36]   No matter what the Constitution says, the
President is held responsible for disaster and so, Truman felt, "a
successful administration is one of strong presidential leadership.
Weak leadership—or no leadership—produces failure, often disaster."[37]

In January, 1947, without explanation Truman presented his annual
message in person, a procedure which he followed thereafter until
1953. The Full Employment Act of 1946 now made it an additional
presidential duty to present a national production and employment
budget based on studies by the Council of Economic Advisers. Thus,
he presented a 7,000 word "state of the union" address (the first ever
televised), a 30,000 word written Economic Report, and a Budget
Message of 1,626 pages.

The format of the Truman addresses was unlike that of Wilson
and Roosevelt; he favored the lengthy, detailed, survey-type of
yearly report which literally tried to review the many facets of the
"state of the union."   Boldness of language and program often were
blunted by the sheer weight of items included for mention. James
Reston criticized the 1948 address for its lack of direction and labeled
it, "not a speech but a catalogue." [38]   In 1952 the *New York Times*
apparently yearned for a return to the personalized annual message:
"Unfortunately, Mr. Truman lacks the inspired eloquence and the
personal magnetism that could be usefully employed in such times
as this to pull all groups and all factions together in heroic fashion
for a common effort. His premises are sound enough, but this message loses its way among side-issues and inconsequences. Mr. Truman has thrown into this message a great variety of recommendations,
some of which have no direct connection with the central problem
now before us."[39]

The President's decision not to stand for re-election in 1952 led
to speculation about the fate of the "state of the union" message
for January, 1953. Here would be the situation which Roosevelt
foresaw of a "lame duck" President addressing a newly elected Congress.   There was some thought that Truman might forego his
message and allow its function to be at least partially fulfilled by
the inaugural address of the incoming President. The perplexity
was resolved when he sent a written message, using the method broadly suggested earlier by F.D.R.: "On previous occasions it has been my
custom to set forth proposals for legislative action in the coming
years. But that is not my purpose today. The presentation of a
legislative program falls properly to my successor, not to me, and
I would not infringe upon his responsibility to chart the forward

course. Instead, I wish to speak of the course we have been following the past 8 years and the position at which we have arrived."[40]

The message was in effect a Farewell Address. Over twice the
length of the usual Truman message, the document devoted almost
one-fourth of its 10,000 words to a survey of the milestones in the
President's eight year foreign and domestic record. The rest of
the message dealt, in Truman's words, with an examination and
analysis of the "overriding questions of our times."

The content of the Truman annual messages was panoramic. Domestic issues dominated his first ones giving way increasingly to
foreign affairs after the outbreak of war in Korea. The President's
economic program was conveniently summarized in 1947:

"First, promotion of greater harmony between labor and management.

"Second, restriction of monopoly and unfair business practices;
assistance to small business; and the promotion of the free competitive system of private enterprise.

"Third, continuation of an aggressive program of home construction.

"Fourth, the balancing of the budget in the next fiscal year, and
the achieving of a substantial surplus to be applied to the reduction
of the public debt.

"Fifth, protection of a fair level of return to farmers in postwar
agriculture."[41]

By 1949 Truman was President "in his own right" and that year's
address contained a vigorous demand for the enactment of a domestic
program which had become familiar to the nation from the rear-
platform of his "whistle-stop" railroad caravan. Some thirty separate
and distinct recommendations were made. This message also provided the "Fair Deal" appellation for the Truman policies which
had previously been dubbed the "Re-Deal" or the "Truman New
Deal." The christening was based on one of the President's concluding sentences: "I hope for co-operation from farmers, from
labor, and from business. Every segment of our population and
every individual have a right to expect from our Government a fair
deal."

Truman recognized that domestic and foreign affairs had grown
virtually interdependent; in 1949 he said, "Our domestic programs
are the foundations of our foreign policy." In 1951 he went even
further, "Indeed, the state of our Nation is in great part the state
of our friends and allies throughout the world. The gun that points

at them points at us also." His three-point "practical, realistic program of action" to meet the challenge of Soviet aggression called
for: extended economic assistance where it could be effective, continued military assistance to countries that wanted to defend themselves, and a continued effort to work for peaceful settlements of
international disputes.

The President's assessment of the 1952 "state of the union" was
a somber one:

"First: The threat of world war is still very real. . . . If you don't
think the threat of Communist armies is real, talk to some of our
men back from Korea.

"Second: If the United States had to try to stand alone against
a Soviet-dominated world, it would destroy the life we know and
the ideals we hold dear. Our allies are essential to us, just as we
are essential to them. . . .

"Third: The things we believe in most deeply are under relent-
less attack. We have the responsibility of saving the basic moral
and spiritual values of our civilization." [42]

In less than fifty years the United States had moved from the
wings to the center of the world stage; a stage which was broaden-
ing and eliminating "wing space." New subjects represented the
shift in position: Marshall Plan, "Point Four," Voice of America,
international relief and displaced persons, the United Nations, Rio
De Janeiro Treaty, international control of the atom. Former stars
in the annual message show—Indian affairs, civil service, immigration,
public lands, boundary disputes—had been relegated to lesser roles,
"bit parts."

"The overriding question of our time," President Truman asserted
in his valedictory message, was whether the world could build a
future of world peace or whether it was drifting toward a holocaust
of atomic war. The advent of atomic energy, he said, had so transformed the nature of war that a total struggle between the free
nations and the Soviet Empire "might dig the grave not only of
our Stalinist opponents but of our own society, our world as well
as theirs." [43] The concluding paragraphs of the message featured
the so-called "containment policy," although not identified as such
by the President:

"As we continue to confound Soviet expectations, as our world
grows stronger, more united, more attractive to men on both sides
of the iron curtain, then inevitably there will come a time of change
within the Communist world. We do not know how that change

will come about, whether by deliberate decision in the Kremlin, by coup d'etat, by revolution, by defection of satellites, or perhaps by some unforeseen combination of such factors as these.

"But if the Communist rulers understand they cannot win by war, and if we frustrate their attempts to win by subversion, it is not too much to expect their world to change its character, moderate its aims, become more realistic and less implacable, and recede from the cold war they began."

In the 1952 campaign Republican nominee Dwight D. Eisenhower was extremely critical of President Truman's past attacks on Congress: "You cannot take the great legislative body that is, after all, the United States and speaks for the population, and ignore it, make fun of it, go up and down the countryside talking about it in derogatory terms."[44] He brought to the presidency a genuine respect for the legislators and a firm belief in the separation of powers doctrine. His first year in office consisted of cautious tactics based on friendly persuasion and patience. His actions suggested to one observer, the constitutional monarch bent on setting and maintaining a moral tone and approving decisions made by department heads.[45] After one year in office, however, Eisenhower began to take a firmer tone and a more resolute approach as a result of his disappointment with the way Congress had responded to his program. In July, 1954, Cabell Phillips, in a story headlined, "President Is Finding Firmer Line Pays Off," reported that "President Eisenhower has drawn a pair of brass knucks over the kid gloves with which he has been handling Congress in the past." Mr. Phillips referred to the President's "unaccustomed candor" in defending his health insurance bill as "almost Trumanesque—for a President who has spent the first eighteen months of his Administration gingerly avoiding even the suspicion of infringement upon the separate and co-ordinate powers of Congress."[46]

Increasingly after 1954 it seemed clear that Eisenhower was moving toward a more vigorous exercise of presidential prerogatives. At a 1956 press conference he wanted it understood that he intended to work for the enactment of his recommendations and he was not making them "to pass the time away or to look good. . . . He was going to work for their enactment. Make no mistake about that. That was exactly what he was in the White House for and what he intended to do."[47] By 1960 it seemed a safe bet, however, that Eisenhower would not go down in history as a "strong" President. In a sense, he had reversed Jefferson; he strengthened the presidency but weakened his own personal power by dispersing authority in the executive branch. The result is what Edward S. Corwin calls the "institution-alized presidency": the cabinet is employed as an "instrument of collective policy-making . . . each member is expected to assume full responsibility for the conduct of the affairs of his department. . . . Each of these gentlemen, according to the President, is an independent officeholder with his own views of appropriate policy, with which the President has no warrant to interfere." [48]

At his first official cabinet meeting, Eisenhower expressed doubt that a "state of the union" message could be gathered together which would justify calling Congress into joint session. The decision was, however, to go ahead, and on February 2, 1953 he came before Congress less than one month after Truman had sent his annual message. Eisenhower explained that the time in which his administration had been in office had been "too brief to permit preparation of a detailed and comprehensive program of recommended action" and that such a program would be forthcoming in the weeks ahead, after appropriate study; "Today can provide only a sure and substantial beginning." [49] The message of over 8,000 words, which took fifty-seven minutes to read—the longest oral presentation yet of the "state of the union" series[50]—ranged over a variety of subjects in the foreign and domestic areas enumerating details and sketching general programs for congressional consideration. His comment, "there are many important subjects of which I make no mention today," did not alter the fact that the new President had given his listeners a comprehensive rather than a selective survey.

Subsequent Eisenhower annual messages have followed the form laid down by the first one. Basically they have been compendia; long on documentation, short on dramatization, and more like shotgun blasts which pepper the target than like sniper shots which strike at the bull's-eye with greater force and effect. This approach was popular with the Republican Presidents of the 1920's and also, to a lesser degree, Truman, but is in sharp contrast to the carefully aimed appeals of Wilson and F.D.R.

Although he continued to present the yearly message in person, Eisenhower apparently had no fixed notions about the desirability or necessity of this procedure. He is reported as having asked, at a cabinet meeting on December 3, 1954, whether he should, as in the previous year, deliver the message in person. He was persuaded that it was very important to do so.[51] In January, 1956 Eisenhower was still recovering from a heart attack of the year before and therefore sent a written message to Congress. Presidential assistant Sherman Adams had requested concise departmental reports because, he said, the President had once voiced the hope that he would someday deliver a twenty minute annual address.[52] The resulting message, however, was another 7,500 word catalogue of information and recommendations for the legislators. Eisenhower did enliven public interest in the message, however, by having a seven-minute personal summary of it recorded and filmed at Key West where he was recuperating. This presidential commentary, presented on radio and television, explained that the message to Congress was a long document which contained "a review of the accomplishments of the past three years, as well as many recommendations for the further advancement of our country in the years to come."

A year later Eisenhower was well enough to resume the oral presentation of the annual message. He cut the delivery time to thirty-three minutes but it was still a discursive address. The keynote was a call for continuity; a "moderate, modest, muted" message, Roscoe Drummond called it, "with no appeal to the political grandstand . . . authentic Eisenhower in mood and substance."[53] Coming as it did five days after the President's appearance before Congress to ask for a "free hand" in the Middle East, the 1957 "state of the union" report was somewhat anti-climactic. But then, none of the Eisenhower annual messages had ever "struck fire." The New York Times which had formerly favored the dramatically focused address experienced an editorial change of heart, in 1954, apparently in sympathetic recognition of changing times. It accepted the Eisenhower compendium approach as necessary because "those days are gone forever when the problems were fairly simple and the President could give the 'state of the union' in a few hundred words."[54]

A month and a half before his 1958 annual message was due Eisenhower suffered a slight stroke. A month later the New York Times reported that the White House was considering an innovation: the President would deliver a ten minute "curtain raiser" and let the reading clerks finish up delivering the message.[55] Nothing came of the idea, however; on January 9, 1958 Eisenhower stood before Congress and gave his usual over forty-five minute rendition of his usual over 5,000 word message.

Editorial comment was almost unanimous in cheerfully acknowledging the vigor and stamina of the President. Not so unanimous was the comment about the effectiveness of his address. The Herald Tribune

shouted its editorial approval across the front page, calling it a
"Great Speech," but the *New York Times* editorially felt that "What
the speech most lacked was a sense of urgency and inspiration at a
critical moment in American history" and its news column reported
that "The most general criticism even from those who liked the tone
of the message, was that Mr. Eisenhower used too broad a brush in
presenting his program . . . " [56] The address promised at the outset to
focus on "two tasks confronting us that so far outweigh all others that
I shall devote this year's message to them." The first was "to insure
safety through strength" and the second "to do the constructive work
of building a peace." The itemized outline of eight areas requiring
action had its predictable effect of losing its impact on a rapidly tiring
audience. It was too much to digest at one sitting.

Again in 1959 and 1960 the President appeared before Congress
and spoke for upwards of forty-five minutes. Allen Drury's report in
1959 applied equally to both occasions: "Looking somewhat relieved,
the President departed; looking somewhat bored the Senate withdrew . . . No one obviously had expected surprises; no one obviously
had been surprised." [57]

The main theme of most of the Eisenhower annual messages was
starkly put in 1958: "The threat to our safety, and to the hope of a
peaceful world, can be simply stated. It is Communist imperialism."
The generalized aim of his administration had been set forth in his
first yearly report in 1953:

"Application of America's influence in world affairs with such forti-
tude and such foresight that it will deter aggression and eventually
secure peace;

"Establishment of a national administration of such integrity and
such efficiency that its honor at home will ensure respect abroad;

"Encouragement of those incentives that inspire creative initiative
in our economy, so that its productivity may fortify freedom everywhere; and

"Dedication to the well-being of all our citizens and to the attain-
ment of equality of opportunity for all, so that our Nation will ever
act with the strength of unity in every task to which it is called." [58]

Highlights of the message were the announcement that the American seventh fleet would no longer prevent landings from Formosa on
the Chinese mainland, that the first order of business for the new
administration would be a balanced budget, that the executive branch
would assume primary responsibility for keeping disloyal and danger-

ous employees out of its departments, and that the President would use his authority to end segregation in the District of Columbia, including the federal government, as well as in the Armed Forces.

The 1954 message divided itself between domestic and foreign affairs but the overlapping nature of the two was pointed out by the President: "We now turn to matters which are normally characterized as domestic, well realizing that what we do abroad affects every problem at home—from the amount of taxes to our very state of mind." [59] Two recommendations, found surprising by the *New York Times*, were loss of United States citizenship for anyone convicted of advocating the violent overthrow of the American government; and a proposed constitutional amendment to permit voting at the age of eighteen. [60]

The 1955 message was very largely a repetition of the one before. The most important new items called for the creation of a Reserve training program to supplement the new draft act, a federal minimum wage law of ninety cents per hour, and a program of federal aid to meet the great shortage of public school classrooms. The President also felt that the federal government should give more official recognition to cultural activities; he recommended the establishment of a federal advisory commission on the arts, and a system of merit awards.

The message received a mixed reception in Congress. Many Democrats found little to complain about; some members of the President's own party felt that the address could just as well have been delivered by a Democratic chief executive. Most editorial comment agreed that it was "moderately progressive." Eisenhower provided the best example of the course which he would have the federal government follow:

"The aspirations of most of our people can best be fulfilled through their own enterprise and initiative, without Government interference. This administration, therefore, follows two simple rules: First, the Federal Government should perform an essential task . . . only when it cannot otherwise be adequately performed; and, second, in performing that task, our Government must not impair the self-respect, the freedom and the incentive of the individual. So long as these two rules are observed, the Government can and must fully meet its obligations without creating a dependent population or a domineering bureaucracy." [61]

In 1956 and 1957 the annual messages continued in the same vein. Arthur Krock charged the President with taking a "leaf from the Democrat's book" in 1956 when Eisenhower promised, in Krock's words, "federal aid in many New and Fair Deal directions." [62] The following year the *New York Times* headlined its "News of the Week" commentary on the annual message: "Eisenhower Embraces More of the New Deal; Still Conservative at Heart, He Bows to the Prevailing Trend." [63] The messages ran the gamut of presidential overview. It was estimated that at least forty-six separate legislative actions, not including appropriation bills, would have been needed to carry the recommended 1956 program into effect. [64]

The 1957 address allotted equal space to foreign and domestic matters. While an "unprecedented peak in our economic prosperity" was reported, Eisenhower emphasized inflationary dangers. The message differed from previous ones in the scarcity of specific recommendations; basic administration policy was affirmed and no major new proposals were advanced. The President seemed content to till the land which had already been laid out rather than break new ground. His "safety through strength" 1958 message called for an eight point program: reorganization of the Defense department, an accelerated defense effort, more effective foreign aid, increased foreign trade, exchange of atomic secrets with the Allies, increased spending for education and research, maintenance of a balanced budget, and closer co-operation with the Russians on projects like the "science for peace" program. By 1959 the President was reporting on a defense "hardware" which would have astounded General Washington:

"National security programs account for nearly 60 percent of the entire Federal budget for this coming year. . . . The overall cost of introducing Atlas into our Armed Forces will average $35 million per missile on the firing line. This year we are investing an aggregate of close to $7 billion in missile programs alone. . . . Our latest atomic submarines will cost $50 million each, while some special types cost three times as much.

"We are now ordering fighter aircraft which are priced at 50 times as much as the fighters of World War II. We are buying certain bombers that cost their weight in gold, exactly." [65]

In January, 1960 President Eisenhower, in what was probably his last in person annual message presentation, succinctly gave his view of the "state of the world": "With both sections of this divided world in possession of unbelievably destructive weapons, mankind approaches a state where mutual annihilation becomes a possibility. No other fact of today's world equals this in importance—it colors everything we say, plan, and do." More routinely, the chief executive did what many others before him had done when he hailed the entry of a new state— Hawaii. His announced intention of presenting to Congress a balanced budget suggested that at least one recommendation had made the passage from the eighteenth to the twentieth century. The Eisenhower "middle way" philosophy of government was spelled out in all of the annual messages; perhaps most eloquently in the concluding paragraph of his first annual address to Congress:

"There is, in world affairs, a steady course to be followed between an assertion of strength that is truculent and a confession of helplessness that is cowardly.

"There is, in our affairs at home, a middle way between untrammeled freedom of the individual and the demands for the welfare of the whole Nation. This way must avoid government by bureaucracy as carefully as it avoids neglect of the helpless.

"In every area of political action, freemen must think before they can expect to win.

"In this spirit must we live and labor: confident of our strength, compassionate in our heart, clear in our mind. In this spirit, let us together turn to the great tasks before us." [66]

When Russell Baker reported in his *New York Times* account of Eisenhower's 1960 annual address that the "State of the Union messages have historically been sleep inducers," he could not have been including those of Franklin Roosevelt. The dull, all-embracing message never appealed to F.D.R. Endowed with a talent for coining memorable phrases, gifted with a magnificent radio voice, and animated with a zest for public life, he imparted an unmatched style of freshness and informality to the annual reports. In 1936, after extolling the virtues of co-operation in the Western Hemisphere, the President observed, "The rest of the world—Ah! There is the rub." In 1937 he summarized economic ills: "Overproduction, underproduction and speculation are three evil sisters who distill the troubles of unsound inflation and disastrous deflation." In 1940 he hoped that "we shall have fewer American ostriches in our midst. It is not good for the ultimate health of even ostriches to bury their heads in the sand." The obvious play for popular appeal is typified by the President's warning in 1941 that, "We must especially beware of that small group of selfish men who would clip the wings of the American eagle in order to feather their own nest." His remark in 1943 that "Washington may be a madhouse—but only in the sense that it is the Capital City of a Nation which is fighting mad," is further evidence of a style verve which never before or since has been permitted to enliven the presidential messages. Conversely, Roosevelt reached pinnacles of eloquence in the same addresses, often almost cheek by jowl with the "folksiest" utterances. The enunciation of the "Four Freedoms" in 1941 is an example of this versatility:

"The first is freedom of speech and expression—everywhere in the world.

"The second is freedom of every person to worship God in his own way—everywhere in the world.

"The third is freedom from want — which, translated into world terms means economic understandings which will secure to every nation a healthy peacetime life for its inhabitants—everywhere in the world.

"The fourth is freedom from fear—which, translated into world terms means a world-wide reduction of armaments to such a point and in such a thorough fashion that no nation will be in a position to commit an act of physical aggression against any neighbor—anywhere in the world.

"That is no vision of a distant millennium. It is a definite basis for a kind of world attainable in our own time and generation." [67]

His preference for the pronoun, "I," stands out in marked contrast to all other Presidents except the earlier Roosevelt. His obvious pleasure in and effective use of repetitive phraseology has been credited to the influence of the poet Walt Whitman. [68] F.D.R.'s 1936 message, for example, contained a spirited challenge to his political enemies which took the form of a long series of questions:

"Shall we say to the farmer, . . .

"Shall we say to the home owners, . . .

"Shall we say to the several millions of unemployed, . . .

"Shall we say to the needy unemployed, . . .

"Shall we say to the children who have worked all day, . . .

"Shall we say to the laborer, . . .

"Shall we say to the unemployed and the aged, . . .

"Shall we say to the men and women who live in conditions of squalor, . . . [69]

Roosevelt more than any other President used familiar passages from the Bible to buttress and illustrate his arguments. In 1936, for example, he accused his detractors as "Autocrats in smaller things, they seek autocracy in bigger things. 'By their fruits ye shall know them.'" In 1941 the President warned, "We must always be wary of those who with sounding brass and a tinkling cymbal preach the 'ism' of appeasement." Some paragraphs later he reminded his listeners that "As men do not live by bread alone, they do not fight by armaments alone." In 1943 the President insisted that "the United Nations can and must remain united for the maintenance of peace by preventing any attempt to rearm in Germany, in Japan, in Italy, or in any other Nation which seeks to violate the Tenth Commandment— 'Thou shalt not covet.'" Many students of Roosevelt's style have commented on his predilection for Biblical phrases. Mrs. Eleanor Roosevelt has said that "His favorite reading was in history and biography. I think, though, that the Bible was the main literary influence on him. He was a student of the Bible, and loved it. He knew all of it very well." [70]

Truman did not possess the ingratiating manner nor the radio appeal of his predecessor and his message style reflected a recognition of these facts. He confided to some newsmen that he did not relish reading a speech in person before Congress: "It is a long chore, and the previous year, after spending forty minutes, Congress had gone ahead and ignored it [1948 annual message]." [71] Furthermore, he had his own idea of what constituted a good speech: "A direct statement of the facts without trimmings and without oratory." [72]

The Truman annual reports were characterized by their serious and conscientious attention to detailed reporting and blueprint-like recommendations. Their somewhat sober tone, however, was sometimes lightened by his extemporaneous comments — typical of Truman's politically-conscious, good-fellow approach to things. In 1946, for example, following the congressional elections which had resulted in Republican majorities the President commented before starting his prepared speech: "It looks like a good many of you have moved over to the left since I was here last."

Eisenhower, similarly, liked to have his little jokes with Congress. He drew a warm non-partisan laugh in 1960 when he reminded the lawmakers that "I am not unique as a President in having worked with a Congress controlled by the opposition party — except that no other President ever did it for quite so long."[73] As a rule, however, Eisenhower undertook his duty to report with soldierly seriousness. He favored the numerical listing of hard core factual information; an approach which was supported by his plainspoken, straightforward, concise, businesslike style of speaking. Rhetoric and argumentation which were so integral a part of the Roosevelt flare were conspicuously absent with the General-President. Some exceptions were noticeable as in 1958 when Eisenhower argued in favor of his mutual aid program: "This is no 'giveaway.' Let's stick to facts. We cannot afford to have one of our most essential security programs shot down with a slogan." And in 1960 when he cautioned:

"The fissure that divides our political planet is deep and wide. We live, moreover, in a storm of semantic disorder in which old labels no longer faithfully describe.

"Police states are called 'people's democracies.' Armed conquest of free people is called 'liberation.' Such slippery slogans make difficult the problem of communicating true faith, facts, and beliefs." [74]

Under Truman and Eisenhower the annual message style bogged down under the heavy weight of specific legislative items. The preparation of the annual message in 1948 is typical of the postwar period:

"President Truman himself laid down the outline of the message before a word was written. The message evolved through several drafts under the supervision of the President's legal counselor and his personal legislative assistant and then went back to the President for comments. President Truman went over the final drafts, sentence by sentence, determining final choice of words and of emphasis. Twenty-five of the eighty-three legislative items gathered by the Legislative Service of the Budget Bureau appeared in the finished draft of the State of the Union Message." [75]

As a consequence of the greater emphasis on details, literary flourishes have all but vanished from the post-F.D.R. messages except in the opening and closing paragraphs where Truman and Eisenhower relaxed from the frantic business of literally giving full information to Congress on the "state of the union." In 1959, for example, the President's itemized speech was capped by this non-mundane vision: "If we make ourselves worthy of American ideals, if we do not forget that our Nation was founded on the premise that all men are creatures of God's making, the world will come to know that it is free men who carry forward the true promise of human progress and dignity."

This paragraph also illustrates the new trend since 1934 of including religious mention in the annual message. Franklin Roosevelt invariably made some reference to divine providence, as in the last words of his final report: "We pray that we may be worthy of the unlimited opportunity that God has given us." [76] Harry Truman brought religious thanksgiving back to the popularity it had enjoyed one hundred years earlier; each of his eight annual messages showed Mr. Truman at his old-fashioned, God-fearing-American best—as, for example, in 1949:

"I am confident that the Divine Power which has guided us to this time of fateful responsibility and glorious opportunity will not desert us now.

"With the help from Almighty God which we have humbly acknowledged in every turning point in our national life we shall be able to perform the great tasks which He now sets before us." [77]

The tendency of the Presidents in wartime or "cold war" periods to extol the virtues of their side and to stress the evilness of the enemy cropped up again in 1941-1945 and during the Korean War and its aftermath. On January 6, 1942 Roosevelt explained World War II in these terms:

"Our enemies are guided by brutal cynicism, by unholy contempt for the human race. We are inspired by a faith that goes back through all the years to the first chapter of the Book of Genesis: 'God created man in His own image.'

". . . No compromise can end that conflict. There never has been— there never can be — successful compromise between good and evil. Only total victory can reward the champions of tolerance, and decency, and freedom, and faith." [78]

Eisenhower, after working a long time in preparing his 1955 annual message, is reported to have concluded that "all he had to recommend could be related to the basic issues of good and evil about which he was so much concerned." [79] The basic issue at stake, the message declared, was not economic or governmental or military; it was "the true nature of man. Either man is the creature whom the Psalmist described as 'a little lower than the angels' crowned with glory and honor, holding 'dominion over the works' of his Creator; or man is a soulless, animated machine to be enslaved, used and consumed by the state for its own glorification." [80]

All of his annual messages included some religious reference; one of the most spirited ones came in 1958 when after having denounced "Communist imperialism," he concluded that mankind "will see more clearly than ever that the future belongs, not to the concept of the regimented atheistic state, but to the people—the God-fearing peace-loving people of all the world."

The period since 1932 with its paralyzing depression and cataclysmic wars would indeed raise questions even in the mind of the most confirmed optimist—which is what most of the Presidents have been. The realities, however, of the twentieth century put a damper on the confident nineteenth century philosophy which proclaimed progress to be inevitable, a law of nature. F.D.R. reversed the "glad tidings" messages of the 1920s, substituting a report which almost seemed to delight in calling public attention to shortcomings in the American system. The critical analysis was the opening wedge; a suggested program of action followed and the final paragraphs concluded on a high and sustained note of optimism and confidence. Perhaps the best example is the 1941 address which warned that this annual message was unique in American history because the United States had never before had its security as seriously threatened as it was that day. Yet, some 3,000 words later, Roosevelt assured his audience that "there can be no end save victory" as a reward for their support of other free nations.

He was supremely confident of his ability to lead; he never failed to keep a constant series of goals and objectives before the public. Arthur Krock noted an exception in 1940: "For the first time in years he [Roosevelt] did not sound a trumpet-call for some kind of bitter controversy with all those, whatever their party affiliation, who have questioned the New Deal." [81]

Truman followed the Roosevelt plan of attack. Increasingly after 1948, he used a realistic appraisal of the darker side of the "state of the union" as a springboard for launching programs of domestic reform. In 1952 he actually referred to the record of the past year in terms of a credit and debit side of a ledger; and, in 1949, after a deep bow in the direction of American capitalism, Truman went on to catalogue failures of the system with a candor hardly equaled in the long history of the yearly reports:

"We are suffering from excessively high prices.

"Our production is still not large enough to satisfy our demands.

"Our minimum wages are far too low.

"Small business is losing ground to growing monopoly.

"Our farmers still face an uncertain future. . . .

"Some of our natural resources are still being wasted. We are acutely short of electric power. . . .

"Five million families are still living in slums and firetraps. . . .

"Our health is far behind the progress of medical science. . . .

"Our schools, in many localities, are utterly inadequate.

"Our democratic ideals are often thwarted by prejudice and intolerance." [82]

Eisenhower, on the other hand, has had hardly ought but good to say about the "state of the union." In 1954 his audience was assured at the outset that "Much for which we may be thankful has happened during the past year"; a documentation of the President's assertion followed for most of the remaining message. Examples and references to national trouble spots were small in number, almost lost in the long, comprehensive report. The 1955 message, pitched in the same tone of trust and certainty, brought reactions in New York newspapers varying from "Amens" to caustic gibes. The *Herald Tribune* commented editorially, "The State of the Union is good; and in all humility and thankfulness the people should be ready to recognize this fact." The *Daily News* doubted that anyone was wildly excited about the President's address; and the *New York Post* entitled its editorial, "Not Much Doing Today, Folks." [88]

The next year, an election one, the President saw the country at peace, the security posture commanding respect, the economy at an unparalleled level of prosperity, and as a people, "achieving ever higher standards of living—earning more, producing more, consuming more, building more, and investing more than ever before." Eisenhower reported that the national income was "more widely and fairly distributed than ever before" and "Virtually all sectors of our society [were] sharing in these good times." But, half-way through his report, he did acknowledge that "Our farm people are not sharing as they should in the general prosperity." The President emphasized the need for wisdom and vision and resolution but the message was clearly no call for alarm.

In 1958 Eisenhower prefaced his annual message with the frank proposition that: "I am not here to justify the past, gloss over the problems of the present, or propose easy solutions for the future. I am here to state what I believe to be right and what I believe to be wrong; and to propose action for correcting what I think wrong." What the President believed to be "right," however, far outnumbered what he believed to be "wrong." The "state of the union" was in good shape: "If our history teaches us anything, it is this lesson: so far as the economic potential of our Nation is concerned, the believers in the future of America have always been the realists. I count myself as one of this company." One allowance of an administration shortcoming was permitted when Eisenhower admitted that "most of us did not anticipate the psychological impact upon the world of the launching of the first earth satellite." But a sentence later his listeners were assured that "As with our military potential, our economic assets are more than equal to the task."

One year later the President was still generally content: "The marked forward thrust of our economy reaffirms our confidence in competitive enterprise." His next annual message continued the same theme: "Today our surging strength is apparent to everyone; 1960 promises to be the most prosperous year in our history." This glowing prospect, however, was immediately followed by a concession which was unusual for the Eisenhower annual messages:

"Yet we continue to be afflicted by nagging disorders.

"Among our current problems that require solution participated in by citizens as well as Government are—

"The need to protect the public interest in situations of prolonged labor-management stalemate;

"The persistent refusal to come to grips with a critical problem in one sector of American agriculture;

"The continuing threat of inflation, together with the persisting tendency toward fiscal irresponsibility;

"In certain instances the denial to some of our citizens of equal protection of the law." [84]

Most blunt for Eisenhower was his open scolding of Congress in 1959 for its failure to act on his recommendations for legislation in the labor-management field. He reminded the lawmakers that "The McClellan committee disclosures of corruption, racketeering, and abuse of trust and power in labor-management affairs have aroused America and amazed other people." Further he cautioned Congress that the world is "watching our conduct" and that "The image of America abroad is not improved when schoolchilden, through closing of some of our schools and through no fault of their own, are deprived of their opportunity for an education." When stirred he threw some thunderbolts but mainly the sun shone bright on his union landscape.

The changing nature of the presidency has been reflected in certain innovations in the annual message content. Since 1934 the yearly report often openly recognizes the existence of poltical parties; a fact scarcely hinted at before. Truman, for example, in 1953 referred to the approaching inauguration of Mr. Eisenhower and pledged his support to the new President. In 1954 Eisenhower acknowledged the party system when he made a bid for support of his legislative program: "All branches of this Government—and I venture to say both our great parties—can support the general objectives of the recommendations I make today, for that objective is the building of a stronger America."

Along with this admission of political realities has come a more bipartisan preparation of the message itself, although final and controlling responsibility has naturally remained with the President. In January, 1954, Eisenhower invited all Democratic congressional leaders to join Republican bigwigs at the White House to hear a reading of the annual message on the day before its delivery at the Capitol. Roosevelt and Truman, on occasion, had provided some advance notice to the Republicans, but it was felt that Eisenhower's policy went further. Arthur Krock's story was headlined: "Eisenhower Makes a Bid at Bipartisan Policy, By Inviting Democrats to Preview on State of the Union Message, He Goes Beyond Predecessors." [85]

Following the congressional elections of 1954, the bipartisan approach was advanced more significantly when the President invited leaders of both parties to the White House on December 14th to discuss questions of foreign policy, mutual security and national defense at a time when the annual message was being prepared for its delivery to Congress a month later. Officials from the appropriate executive departments explained the administration proposals and a general discussion was held on each subject. [86]

Some resentment among the legislators has naturally resulted from the growing pre-eminence of the presidency. Just as naturally, recent Presidents have been uniformly cordial to their lawmakers, favoring them with warm greetings in the annual message. In 1934 F.D.R. flatteringly compared the Seventy-third Congress to the First Congress of 1789; and eleven years later, he was still holding out the peace pipe: "I myself want to tell you, the Members of the Senate and of the House of Representatives, how happy I am in our relationships and friendships. I have not yet had the pleasure of meeting some of the new Members in each House, but I hope that opportunity will offer itself in the near future." [87]

Truman—in spite of his vituperative campaign attacks against the Eightieth Congress—and Eisenhower continued in a similar vein to court congressional favor. If diplomatic language was the rule where Congress was concerned, a similar restraint was noticeably absent in references to the Soviet Union and Communism in the messages since 1946. The remarks by Jackson in 1834 which had been the alleged reason for France's breaking off diplomatic relations were mild asides when compared to the brickbats tossed at the Russians. It is probably true, as one political scientist has suggested, that the language currently being used "may actually contribute to the cause of international peace by making ridiculous the extravagances of wounded *amourpropre* that old-time diplomats habitually affected." [88]

Today, of course, no one (except, perhaps the diplomats) seriously considers the annual message as being merely a report from the chief executive of one branch to another branch of the federal government.

In his final message, Truman referred to one part as being addressed to Premier Stalin in particular. In 1958 after having enumerated the ways in which the Soviets were "waging total cold war," Eisenhower explicitly transcended his congressional audience: "My last call for action is not primarily addressed to the Congress and people of the United States. Rather it is a message from the people of the United States to all other peoples, especially those of the Soviet Union." The treatment given to his 1954 address is indicative of its current circulation. The U.S. Information Agency transmitted it around the world. The Voice of America broadcast the full text to an English language audience estimated at about 45,000,000. Highlights of the address were carried in 33 languages. Moreover, the text was transmitted by wireless to 57 U.S.I.A. overseas posts for distribution to some 10,000 foreign publications.[89]

The advent of television has resulted in the addition of a White House staff consultant who, on occasion, has made suggestions concerning the presidential wardrobe, style of reading glasses, and speaking posture—all designed to enhance the chief executive's 'public image'."[90] Some customs associated with the annual message have survived the abrasive factors of the 170 years of usage. The President still attends the customary church service which is held on the opening day of Congress. No more, however, is there the ceremonial journey of the silk-hatted committees from Capitol to White House to notify the President that Congress is ready to receive his message. Not since Wilson's illness forced a change in procedure has a committee gone in person to see the chief executive; an informal telephone conversation has been substituted. In recent years even this method has not always been followed. In 1930 the *New York Times* reported that "In the past two years the congressional committee has merely idled in the cloakroom for a few moments, then returned to announce the date of the President's message."[91] In 1956 when Eisenhower was recuperating in Florida he was notified by telephone that Congress was organized and ready to transact business; he assured the committees that his annual message would be transmitted for reading by congressional clerks. The mode and manner of delivery have differed but there has been perfect agreement in the surety with which the presidential annual message has greeted the opening sessions of every Congress.

Chapter Eight

EPILOGUE

"The President-elect is about to take up the greatest burdens, the most compelling responsibilities, given to any man," said President Truman in his final annual message a fortnight before relinquishing his office:

"What are these tasks? The President is Chief of State, elected representative of all the people, national spokesman for them and to them. He is commander in chief of our Armed Forces. He is charged with the conduct of our foreign relations. He is Chief Executive of the Nation's largest civilian organization. He must select and nominate all top officials of the executive branch and all Federal judges. And, on the legislative side, he has the obligation and the opportunity to recommend and to approve or veto legislation. Besides all this, it is to him that a great political party turns naturally for leadership, and that, too, he must provide as President.

"This bundle of burdens is unique; there is nothing else like it on the face of the earth. Each task could be a full-time job. Together they would be a tremendous undertaking in the easiest of times. But our times are not easy; they are hard—as hard and complex, perhaps, as any in our history. Now the President not only has to carry on these tasks in such a way that our democracy may grow and flourish and our people prosper, but he also has to lead the whole free world in overcoming the Communist menace—and this under the shadow of the atomic bomb."

This prospectus of the presidential position is not the one envisioned by the constitutional framers. They conceived of a separation of powers in which the primary responsibility for lawmaking rested with Congress; the President's main function was as chief executive and law enforcer. Today the success of a presidency is most likely to be measured by its batting average — how many times at bat and how many hits against the opposition in the legislature. This score-card rating is a twentieth century phenomenon, chiefly the result of the concept championed by Wilson and the two Roosevelts that the President should be the policy setter in legislative matters.

The transposition of the lawmaking initiative to the President was not achieved by steady and uninterrupted gains but rather by an ebb

131

and flow in which the tide has moved in the direction of more prerogatives to the chief executive. It is within this alternating shift of political primacy from Capitol Hill to White House, back and forth, that the function of the annual message has been modified. Washington and John Adams fulfilled their constitutional duty to report and make recommendations in a manner and ceremonial reminiscent of British custom. The message, delivered orally, was relatively nonpartisan and restrained in tone and style. The content struck a balance between factual reporting, general observations, and recommendations with the latter made in a clearly deferential way. Both Houses prepared replies to the addresses and presented them in person at the President's residence.

In 1801 Jefferson substituted the written message for the annual address thereby eliminating the "monarchical" ritual and pomp associated with the occasion. His secretary without escort delivered the communication to the presiding officer of each House and replies were not drafted by Congress. The Jefferson annual messages were similar in composition and length to the preceding ones but with the administration of Madison, the emphasis on factual reporting began to dominate the text. A steady but discontinuous growth in message length continued until Taft cut the yearly report into separate messages and sent them to Congress serially. The bulk of the communication from 1809 to 1912 usually consisted of the summary of cabinet reports. Exceptions to this generalization were the annual messages of Jackson, Lincoln, Johnson, Cleveland, and Theodore Roosevelt; this group of Presidents turned the focus of their reports more upon the public than on Congress and allotted relatively more space to recommendations and the advocacy of presidential policies.

Wilson in 1913 reintroduced the annual address but Congress was asked to omit replies. A new pattern of less inclusive yearly messages was initiated. The attention of the nation was directed dramatically toward a few overriding issues and the personal appearance of the President before the lawmakers assured widespread press coverage. Factual reporting was held to a minimum; commentary defending and projecting presidential proposals dominated Wilson's report on the "state of the union." Harding retained the in person address but favored the kaleidoscopic message with its emphasis on information rather than recommendations, and with its preference for including many subject areas rather than a select few. Coolidge discontinued the oral delivery after one appearance before Congress and led the way back to the written communication with its predilection for spotlighting areas that had been traversed rather than pointing the way which Congress should travel. Hoover followed the Harding-Coolidge pattern of reporting and used the written message exclusively.

In 1934 Franklin D. Roosevelt resurrected the Wilsonian format; oral in delivery and specific in purpose again characterized the annual address. Congress was treated as an incidental audience; the focus was clearly the nation and the world. When illness prevented F.D.R. from presenting in person his "state of the union" assessment in 1944 and 1945, he dispatched written messages to Capitol Hill at noon and gave abbreviated versions at night over the radio. Truman, with the exceptions of his first and final reports, used the address rather than the message. Unlike Roosevelt, however, he preferred a comprehensive survey which was heavy on details and specific recommendations. Dramatic impact was blunted by the concentration of subject matter presented. Eisenhower has relied exclusively on a personal delivery of the annual message except in 1956 when he was recuperating from a heart attack and was forced to communicate with Congress by a written message. His yearly reports have been Truman-like in form: synoptic, conscientiously prepared, and stolidly discharged. The reaction to his 1955 address, as reported in the *New York Times*, reflects an audience-rating of the preponderance of annual messages since 1945:

"The President's speech ran over fifty-five minutes. One school of criticism maintains that no speech can be so long and also be good. When it was thirty minutes gone, interest in the audience was obviously flagging, and from that point the chamber sank into somnolence. Only once was there a moment of laughter . . . but this flicker of gaiety passed as rapidly as it was born, and the atmosphere grew thicker and thicker. At the forty-five minute mark even two Cabinet members looked bored. . . . Ten minutes later it was over. . . . The burden of acting out a ceremony of state was over, and probably with a grateful sigh, both President and Congress turned back to the jobs they do better." [1]

Such had not been the condition when F.D.R. and Wilson were at the rostrum; nor, at an earlier period, when Theodore Roosevelt, Cleveland, Johnson, Lincoln, and Jackson were submitting sharply worded written messages to Congress. The affinity of hard hitting literary style and the "great" and "near great" Presidents reported in a poll of historians,[2] is impressive but not surprising. Outstanding chief executives have stood at the forefront in dealing with the issues of their administrations and have galvanized public opinion in support of their positions. Presidential leadership, according to Edward S. Corwin and Louis W. Koenig, is largely a matter of two factors, personality and opportunity: "The Presidents whose leadership have made a substantial impact have displayed certain qualities in common. They have been men of courage, firmness, flexibility (even opportunism), and manipulative ability. They have been adept at discerning the currents of the time and directing them into constructive channels." [3]

The acceptance of responsibility by most twentieth century Presidents for herding a legislative platform through Congress has resulted in more candor and frankness in the annual message. From 1790 to 1900 one striking characteristic of all but a handful of the yearly reports was the consistent note of confidence and optimism which rang clearly. In the last sixty years, the mode of operation has moved in the direction of a tactic described in 1788 by Richard Henry Lee: "When we want a man to change his condition, we describe it as wretched, miserable, and despised; and we draw a pleasing picture of that which we would have him assume. . . . It is too often the case in political concerns that men state facts not as they are, but as they wish them to be." [4] Admissions of national shortcomings have come more readily from the "reform" Presidents but even they have been careful to balance their "state of the union" account on the favorable side less their administrations be held answerable for the self-confessed difficulties. The chief executive's position as head of a major political party will continue to influence his appraisal of the view from the White House and thereby prevent his annual message from being what the constitutional framers hoped it would be: a dispassionate, non-partisan, institutionalized, national keynoting document. Information to Congress has not been unvarnished; realists will have to continue looking elsewhere for supplemental facts in assessing the "state of the union." The duty of "recommending such measures as he shall judge necessary and expedient" has been expanded since Theodore Roosevelt and Wilson established the role of the President as prime mover in setting up the legislative agenda. "Outcries against 'dictatorship' and 'speeches from the throne' have long been stilled in responsible [congressional] quarters," writes Richard E. Neustadt:

"Indeed, from the congressional point of view, 'service' not domination, is the reality behond these undertakings [special and annual presidential messages]. In practical effect, they represent a means whereby Congress can gain from the outside what comes hard from within: a handy and official guide to the wants of its biggest customer;

an advance formulation of main issues at each session; a work-load ready-to-hand for every legislative committee; an indication, more or less, of what may risk the veto; a borrowing of presidential prestige for most major bills—and thus boosting of publicity-potentials in both sponsorship and opposition."[5]

Since 1945 the annual message has carried more the imprint of the legislative reference division than of the President's personality. It is becoming customary for the yearly address to consume upwards of forty-five minutes and five thousand words in the painstaking enumeration of the memoranda of things to be considered by Congress. This mold of the "state of the union" message form though hardening into contemporary fashionability, need not inhibit oncoming Presidents. The only certainty that characterizes all the messages is the perfect reliability with which each chief executive has obeyed, in one form or another, the duty placed upon him by section 3 of article II. As Neustadt correctly points out, "Past Presidents have focused national attention on their aims by introducing novelties in presentation [of messages]: . . . . Now that all prior innovations have been lumped together into customary practice, what else remains for innovation's sake, than its abandonment? A paradox, perhaps, but paradoxes have been a commonplace in the development of legislative programming."[6]

It seems almost inevitable that the presidency will continue to gain and retain prerogatives and responsibilities in the federal system. In times of crisis Congress has recognized its inability to provide unified leadership and has delegated powers to the President to extricate the nation from difficulties. With the advent of "chronic crisis," more and more people are looking with increased frequency to the White House for direction. "The President is the one man who can get the attention of the American people," writes James Reston. "If he says the nation is in trouble they will listen to him. . . . If he presents programs and legislation to do what he thinks is necessary for the safety of the Republic and explains and keeps explaining why these are essential, he may very well prevail."[7]

The obligation to report to Congress presents a vigorous, purposeful chief executive with a consummate opportunity. For a moment, the world is his stage. How he plays his part will reveal not only his view of the "state of the union" but his concept of the presidency as well.

REFERENCES

CHAPTER ONE

1. James E. Pollard, *The President and the Press* (1958), p. vii.
2. *American Government and Politics* (1935), p. 185.
3. *Sources of the Constitution of the United States* (1927), p. 158.
4. *The American Presidency in Action, 1789* (1948), p. 28.
5. Frederick Ogg, *English Government and Politics* (1936), p. 372.
6. James Harvey Robinson, *The Original and Derived Features of the United States Constitution* (1890), p. 29. Convention speakers were careful to disavow analogy of the American presidency with English royalty. In moving adoption of an executive to consist of a single person James Wilson said that he was not governed by the British model "which was inappliable to the situation of this country." Robinson points out the attention given in the *Federalist Papers* to stress the difference between chief executives in the two countries; it is his conclusion that had the framers taken features from British practice without similar experiences in America, the Constitution would have been rejected.
7. C. C. Thach, *The Creation of the Presidency 1775-1789* (1932), pp. 27-28. Edward S. Corwin says that "The colonial period ended with the belief prevalent that 'the executive magistracy' was the natural enemy, the legislative assembly the natural friend of liberty, a sentiment strengthened by the contemporary spectacle of George III's domination of Parliament." *The President: Office and Powers* (1957), pp. 5-6.
8. Ben P. Poore, *Constitutions* (1877), p. 1335.
9. As reconstructed in Max Farrand, *The Records of the Federal Convention* (1937), III, p. 606.

"In preparing his plan, Charles Pinckney had made extensive use of the Articles of Confederation and of the state constitutions, but of the constitution of New York in particular." Max Farrand, *The Framing of the Constitution* (1913), p. 129.
10. *Ibid.*, p. 160.
11. As reconstructed in Farrand, *The Records of the Federal Convention*, II, p. 185.

Hannis Taylor says that the Pinckney plan was the only "system" actually presented to the Convention and claims that the available documentary evidence shows that the plan was largely used by the Committee of Detail in preparing their draft of the Constitution. *The Origin and Growth of the American Constitution* (1906), p. 36.

C. Perry Patterson asserts that Pinckney and Wilson were responsible for requesting an annual message from the President. "While the Pinckney proposal may have been based on the executive powers provided by the New York constitution, the fact remains that James Wilson, a member of the Committee of Detail . . . used the Pinckney proposal rather than the New York constitution . . . in drafting his suggestions to the committee." *Presidential Government in the United States* (1947), p. 48, note 24.

Alexander Hamilton gave a copy of his plan to Madison at the close of the Convention. It never came formally before the framers and apparently did not influence the final constitutional draft. Article IV, section 10 of the Hamilton plan called for a presidential annual message: "The President at the beginning of every meeting of the Legislature as soon as they shall be ready to proceed to business, shall convene them together at the place where the Senate shall sit, and shall communicate to them all such matters as may be necessary for their information, or as may rquire their consideration. He may by message during the Session communicate all other matters which may to him appear proper." Farrand, *The Record of the Federal Convention*, IV, p. 624.

12. *Ibid.*, II, p. 398.

13. *Ibid.*, II, p. 405.

14. Charles Z. Lincoln, *The Constitutional History of New York* (1906), I, p. 450.

The formality of this period is indicated by a report in the *Council Journal* of 1693. The governor, in completing his address, said: "I leave these things before you for your consideration, which consist of but three heads: Your duty to God, your loyalty and affection to the best of Kings, and your own safety and defense. So, Gentlemen, you may withdraw to your houses. I pray God to direct you to proceed in those things which are most consistent with conscience and honor." The representatives made a bow and withdrew. *Loc. cit.*

15. Ogg, *op. cit.*, p. 372.

16. Lincoln, *op. cit.*, I, p. 450.

17. *Ibid.*, I, p. 576.

CHAPTER TWO

1. James D. Richardson, *Messages and Papers of the President* (1927), I, p. 44. Cited hereafter as Richardson.

2. Charles Warren, *Odd Byways in American History* (1942), p. 137.

3. William Maclay, *Journal* (1927), p. 7.

4. *Ibid.*, pp. 9-10.

5. *Annals of Congress*, I, p. 33.

6. *Ibid.*, p. 333.

7. John C. Fitzpatrick, editor, *The Diaries of George Washington, 1748-1799* (1925), IV, pp. 65-66.

8. *Ibid.*, pp. 67-68.

9. The American Commonwealth (1901), I, p. 57.

10. *Washington and His Colleagues* (1918), pp. 20-21.

Thomas Jefferson, writing in 1814, provides reasons which may have motivated Washington's adherence to British custom: "I do believe that General Washington had not a firm confidence in the durability of our government. He was naturally distrustful of men, and inclined to gloomy apprehensions and I was ever persuaded that a belief that we must at length end in something like a British constitution, had some weight in his adoption of the ceremonies and levees, birthdays, pompous meetings with Congress, and other forms of the same character, calculated to prepare us gradually for a change which he believed possible, and to let it come on with as little shock as might be to the public mind." Quoted in Adrienne Koch and William Peden, editors, *The Life and Selected Writings of Thomas Jefferson* (1944), pp. 175-176.

11. Nathaniel W. Stephenson and Waldo H. Dunn, *George Washington* (1940), p. 274.

12. *The President: Office and Powers*, p. 17.

13. Richardson, I, p. 131.

Norman J. Small quotes Washington as having written to a friend: "It rests with them [Congress] to decide what means ought afterwards to be adopted for promoting the success of the great objects, which I have recommended to their attention." *Some Presidential Interpretations of the Presidency* (1932), p. 163.

14. Washington C. Ford, editor, *The Writings of George Washington* (1893), XI, pp. 502-503.

15. Richardson, I, p. 59.

16. *Ibid.*, I, pp. 130-131.

17. *Ibid.*, I, p. 174.

18. *Ibid.*, I, p. 160.

19. Charles Warren, "Jefferson and the Speech to Congress," *Proceedings of the Massachusetts Historical Society* (1923-1924) LVII, p. 128.

20. *Journal*, p. 171.

21. Quoted in Charles Warren, *Odd Byways in American History*, p. 274.

22. *Ibid.*, p. 150.

23. Richardson, I, p. 132.

24. *Ibid.*, I, p. 160.

25. *Ibid.*, I, p. 282.

26. *Ibid.*, I, p. 244.

Adams argued for protection of American trade: "The commerce of the United States is essential, if not to their [Europe] existence, at least to their comfort, their growth, prosperity, and happiness. The genius, character and habits of the people are highly commercial. Their cities have been formed and exist upon commerce. Our agriculture, fisheries, arts, and manufactures are connected with and depend upon it. In short, commerce has made this country what it is, and it can not be destroyed or neglected without involving the people in poverty and distress. Great numbers are directly and solely supported by navigation. The faith of society is pledged for the preservation of the rights of commercial and seafaring no less than of the other citizens. *Ibid.*, p. 241.

27. *Ibid.*, I, p. 298.

28. Corwin, *op. cit.*, p. 18.

29. The federal debt of precedent in borrowing section 3 of article II was paid back to New York when, in 1821, that state revised its constitution, substituting a written message from the Governor in place of an address. Jefferson's action in 1801 was cited and difficulties arising from the oral presentation were recalled. Peter R. Livingston introduced the amendment and argued, "I had the curiosity once to look over the journals, and I ascertained that it cost $70,000 to the state during ten to fifteen years, in debate about the reply to a governor's speech. This speech is a relic of monarchy, founded in the love of pomp and splendor and show. Besides, when the two houses are of different political character, one approves, the other condemns, the speech; and in 1814 the assembly spent eleven days in discussing the propriety of an answer to the governor's speech, yet we all know that neither a speech nor an answer is legislation. . . .

We have seen, and might see again, a governor on his own carpet, obliged to listen to sentiments which must be odious to him; obliged to submit in quiet to a flagellation, as bitter as political hostility could make it. To be sure, the governor has the last word, and he sends back a reply more bitter, if possible, than the answer; but all this is injudicious and improper, and will be done away by adopting the proposition I have the honor to make." Quoted in Charles Z. Lincoln, *The Constitutional History of New York, I,* pp. 670-671.

30. Richardson, I, p. 313.

31. Charles Warren, "Jefferson and the Speech to Congress," *op. cit.,* p. 172.

32. Woodrow Wilson, *The State* (1889) pp. 565-566; and William Howard Taft, *Our Chief Magistrate* (1916), pp. 39-40.

33. Corwin, *op. cit.,* p. 319, note 40.

34. Small, *op. cit.,* p. 165.

35. *History of the United States* (1893), 1, p. 248.

36. All newspaper commentary on Jefferson's 1801 annual message is taken from quotations in Warren, "Jefferson and the Speech to Congress," *op. cit.,* pp. 123-172.

37. Quoted in Warren, *Odd Byways in American History,* p. 168.

38. Richardson, I, p. 320.

39. *Ibid.,* I, p. 316.

40. "Separated by a wide ocean from the nations of Europe and from the political interests which entangle them together, with productions and wants which render our commerce and friendship useful to them and theirs to us, it can not be to the interest of any to assail us, nor ours to disturb them. We should be most unwise, indeed, were we to cast away the singular blessings of the position in which nature has placed us." *Ibid.,* I, p. 349.

41. *Ibid.,* I, p. 396.

42. *Ibid.,* I, p. 416.

43. *Ibid.,* I, p. 667.

44. *Ibid.,* I, pp. 524-525.

45. *Ibid.,* I, p. 500: "Whilst the benevolent policy of the United States invariably recommended peace and promoted civilization among that wretched portion of the human race, [the Indians] . . . the enemy has not scrupled to call to his aid their ruthless ferocity. . . . In this outrage against the laws of honorable war and against the feelings sacred to humanity the British commander can not resort to a plea of retaliation for it is committed in the face of our example . . . the savages are employed with a knowledge, and even with menaces, that their fury could not be controlled. Such is the spectacle . . . a nation boasting its religion and morality have not been restricted from presenting to an enlightened age."

46. *Ibid.,* I, p. 616.

In 1823 Monroe's analysis of why the United States had prospered gave a surprisingly secular reasoning: "To what, then, do we owe these blessings? It is known to all that we derive them from the excellence of our institutions. Ought we not, then, to adopt every measure which may be necessary to perpetuate them?" *Ibid.,* II, p. 789.

The example of ascribing "national blessings" to other than divine help was not followed by the other pre-Civil War Presidents. John Q. Adams' sentiments expressed in 1828 remained typical: "He has crowned the year with His goodness, imposing on us no other conditions than of improving for our own happiness the blessings bestowed by His hands, and, in the fruition of all His favors, of devoting the faculties with which we have been endowed by Him to His glory and to our own temporal and eternal welfare." *Ibid.*, II, p. 973.

47. *Ibid.*, II, p. 479.

48. The substantive authorship of those parts of the message which became famous as the "Monroe Doctrine" is a matter of dispute among scholars. There is agreement, however, that John Q. Adams contributed many phrases which were later incorporated into the message. James Schouler argues that even if it is true that Monroe borrowed a "phrase, an idea, or an inspiration from any one of his capable cabinet officers, why should he not have historical credit for his courageous pronouncement before Congress and all Europe, upon his solemn responsibility as Chief Executive?" "The Authorship of the Monroe Doctrine," *Annual Report of the American Historical Association* (1905), I, p. 127.

49. Richardson, II, p. 778.

50. *Ibid.*, II, pp. 787-788.

51. *Ibid.*, II, p. 882. Monroe's first annual message reiterated Madison's view that internal improvements were needed but that Congress had no constitutional right to appropriate the money without authorization secured by an amendment.

52. Opposition held up approval and neither of the two appointed delegates reached Panama in time to take part in the meetings.

CHAPTER THREE

1. *New Viewpoints in American History* (1932), p. 218.

2. Vernon Louis Parrington, *Main Currents in American Thought* (1930), II, p. 147.

3. *The President: Office and Powers*, p. 20.

Wilfred E. Binkley states: "Indeed it is scarcely too much to say that by 1825, unless the trend were checked, the presidency bade fair to represent, in time, not much more than a chairmanship for a group of permanent secretaries of the executive department to which Congress at times paid more attention than to the President." *President and Congress* (1947), p. 64.

4. Richardson, III, p. 1471.

5. *Ibid.*, III, pp. 1360-1361.

6. In a letter to the French foreign minister, written the same day, (April 25, 1835), Livingston made a last attempt to restore "mutual good understanding" before being recalled to the United States. His note set forth the official American position concerning the status of the annual message: "The President, as the chief executive power, must have a free and entirely unfettered communication with the coordinate powers of Government. As the organ of intercourse with other nations, he is the only source from which a knowledge of our relations with them can be conveyed to the legislative branches. It results from this that the utmost freedom from all restraints in the details into which he is obliged to enter of international concerns and of the measures in relation to them is essential to the proper performance of this important part of his functions. He must exercise them without having continually before him the fear of offending the susceptibility of the powers whose conduct he is obliged to notice. In the performance of this duty he is subject to public opinion and his own sense of

propriety for an indiscreet, to his constituents for a dangerous, and to his constitutional judges for an illegal, exercise of the power, but to no other censure, foreign or domestic. Were any foreign powers permitted to scan the communications of the Executive, their complaints, whether real or affected, would involve the country in continual controversies; for the right being acknowledged, it would be a duty to exercise it by demanding a disavowal of every phrase they might deem offensive and an explanation of every word to which an improper interpretation could be given. The principle, therefore, has been adopted that no foreign power has a right to ask for explanations of anything that the President, in the exercise of his functions, thinks proper to communicate to Congress, or of any course he may advise them to pursue. This rule is not applicable to the Government of the United States alone, but, in common with it, to all those in which the constitutional powers are distributed into different branches. . . . But whatever may be the principles of other governments, those of the United States are fixed; the right [of foreign government's official protests] will never be acknowledged, and any attempt to enforce it will be repelled by the undivided energy of the nation. I pray your excellency to observe that my argument does not deny a right to all foreign powers of taking proper exceptions to the governmental acts and language of another. It is their interference in all its consultations, in its proceedings while yet in an inchoate state, that we object. Should the President do an official executive act affecting a foreign power, or use exceptional language in addressing it through his ministers or through theirs; should a law be passed injurious to the dignity of another nation—in all these and similar cases a demand for explanation would be respectfully received, and in the manner that justice and a regard to the dignity of the complaining nation would require. *Ibid.*, III, pp. 1397-1399.

7. *Ibid.*, III, p. 1379.

8. Samuel F. Bemis, *A Diplomatic History of the United States* (1942) p. 291. On January 27, 1836, the British government offered to mediate the dispute. Secretary of State Forsyth, in accepting, reiterated the position taken by Livingston in reference to the annual message status. He maintained that the French insistence on an explanation of presidential recommendations to Congress constituted "national interests of the highest order" even surpassing the importance of collecting the debt. Richardson, III, p. 1439.

9. *Ibid.*, III, p. 1341.

10. *Ibid.*, III, p. 1074.

11. Quoted in Corwin, *op. cit.*, p. 322, note 53.

12. Richardson, III, p. 1012.

13. *Ibid.*, III, p. 1021.

14. *Ibid.*, III, p. 1011. The recommendation came to naught. Interestingly in 1836 the Whigs attempted unsuccessfully to defeat Van Buren by nominating "favorite son" candidates in many states hoping thereby to prevent Van Buren from receiving a majority of electoral votes and thus throw the election into the House of Representatives.

15. *Ibid.*, III, pp. 1379-1380.

16. *Ibid.*, IV, pp. 1526-1527.

17. Leonard D. White, *The Jacksonians* (1954), p. 49.

18. Richardson, IV, p. 1828.

19. *Ibid.*, IV, p. 1864.

20. *Ibid.*, VI, p. 2515.

21. *Ibid.*, V, p. 2248.

22. *Ibid.*, V, p. 2351.   By 1848 Polk was saying: "Such will probably be the rapid enlargement of our commerce and navigation and such the addition to the national wealth that the present generation may live to witness the controlling commercial and monetary power of the world transferred from London and other European emporiums to the city of New York." *Ibid.*, V, p. 2493.

23. *Ibid.*, VI, p. 2561.

24. Roy Franklin Nicholas, *Franklin Pierce* (1931), p. 436.

25. Richardson, VI, pp. 2860-2861.

26. *The Congressional Globe* (1855-1856), p. 107.

27. *Ibid.*, p. 107 *ff.*

28. *Ibid.*, p. 113.

29. Richardson, VI, pp. 2882-2883.

30. *Ibid.*, III, p. 1063.

31. *Ibid.*, VII, p. 3158.

32. *Ibid.*, VI, p. 2986.

CHAPTER FOUR

1. Quoted in Edward S. Corwin, *The President: Office and Powers*, p. 324, note 60.   Similar pronouncements were made as President-elect.

2. Wilfred E. Binkley, *President and Congress*, p. 126.   Further, Professor Binkley says, "Unquestionably the high-water mark of the exercise of executive power is found in the administration of Abraham Lincoln."

3. C. Perry Patterson, *Presidential Government in the United States*, p. 121. Lincoln is quoted: "My oath to preserve the Constitution imposed on me the duty of preserving by every indispensible means the government, the nation of which the Constitution was the organic law. . . .   I felt that measures, otherwise unconstitutional, might become lawful by becoming indispensible to the preservation of the Constitution through the preservation of the nation.   Right or wrong, I assumed this ground and now avow it."

4. Quoted in Binkley, *op. cit.*, p. 125.

5. Richardson, VII, p. 3246.

6. *Ibid.*, VII, p. 3332.

7. *Ibid.*, VII, p. 3343.

8. *Ibid.*, VII, p. 3455.

9. *The Use of Presidential Power 1789-1943* (1944), p. 135.

10. Richardson, VII, p. 3338.   In support of his compensated emancipation plan Lincoln predicted that the United States population would be over two hundred and fifty million by 1930. *Ibid.*, VII, p. 3340.

11. *Ibid.*, VII, p. 3456.

12. *George Bancroft* (1944), p. 229.   Professor William A. Dunning, who discovered the Bancroft authorship of the Johnson message, asserts that the "ghost writing" is an interesting more than an important fact.   The significant innovation was Johnson's use of someone outside of his official governmental family since neither the Constitution or law or practice requires that the President personally write his own message.   "More Light on Andrew Johnson," *The American Historical Review* (1906), XI, p. 576.   Dunning thinks that Johnson got outside help on the next three annual messages also; "the evidence

of the papers is that the man who had the least to do with drafting them was Andrew Johnson." p. 583.

The *Nation,* commenting on the Dunning article, made the point: "We are dealing of course with no vulgar question of plagiarism. The problem of authorship, strictly speaking, seldom arises in connection with Presidential messages. They, as a rule, are mosaics; and only the higher critic who can confidently dissect out the documents in the Pentateuch would venture to assign the various bits to the Secretaries, or others, who contributed them." "Authors of Presidential Messages," 82, no. 2118, p. 92.

13. Thaddeus Stevens, Radical leader in the House, stated their position: "He [the President] is the servant of the people as they shall speak through Congress. . . . Andrew Johnson must learn that he is your servant and that as Congress shall order he must obey. There is no escape from it. God forbid that he should have one title of power except that which he derives through Congress and the Constitution." Quoted in Corwin, *op. cit.,* p. 25.

14. Richardson, VIII, p. 3761.

15. *Ibid.,* VIII, p. 3763. In December, 1868, he continued in the same vein: "Abuses which were tolerated during the war for the preservation of the nation will not be endured by the people, now that profound peace prevails. . . . One hundred millions annually are expended for the military force, a large portion of which is employed in the execution of laws both unnecessary and unconstitutional; . . . an army of taxgatherers impoverishes the nation, and public agents, placed by the Congress beyond the control of the Executive, divert from their legitimate purposes large sums of money which they collect from the people in the name of the Government." *Ibid.,* VIII, pp. 3873-3874.

16. *Ibid.,* VIII, p. 3651. 19. *Ibid.,* IX, p. 4109.

17. *Ibid.,* VIII, p. 3875. 20. *Ibid.,* VIII, p. 3992.

18. *Ibid.,* VIII, p. 3889. 21. *Ibid.,* IX, p. 4206.

22. "In nearly every message that I have had the honor of transmitting to Congress I have called attention to the anomalous, not to say scandalous, condition of affairs existing in the Territory of Utah, ... That polygamy should exist in a free, enlightened, and Christian country, without the power to punish so flagrant a crime against decency and morality, seems preposterous . . . what is needed is a law to punish it as a crime, . . . as an institution polygamy should be banished from the land." *Ibid.,* IX, p. 4309.

23. His refutation of the argument that the American type of government would be weakened and destroyed by over-extension might leave Grant open to charges of favoring World Federalism: "Commerce, education, and rapid transit of thought and matter by telegraph and steam have changed all this. Rather do I believe that our Great Maker is preparing the world, in His own good time, to become one nation, speaking one language, and when armies and navies will be no longer required." Richardson, IX, p. 4176.

24. *Ibid.,* IX, p. 4109. 25. Milton, *op. cit.,* p. 137.

26. Richardson, X, p. 4722.

27. *The American Commonwealth,* I, p. 209.

28. Richardson, VIII, p. 3767. 29. *Ibid.,* VIII, p. 3764.

30. *Ibid.,* VIII, p. 3981. 31. *Ibid.,* IX, p. 4288.

32. *Ibid.,* VII, p. 3343. 33. *Ibid.,* VII, p. 3257.

34. *Ibid.,* IX, p. 4353.

35. Grant added: "But I leave comparisons to history, claiming only that I have acted in every instance from a conscientious desire to do what was right, constitutional, within the law, and for the very best interests of the whole people. Failures have been errors of judgment, not of intent." *Ibid.*, IX, p. 4354.

36. Nye, *op. cit.*, p. 297.

CHAPTER FIVE

1. Richardson, X, pp. 4909-4910.

2. Samuel Morison and Henry S. Commager, *The Growth of the American Republic* (1942), II, p. 227.

3. Robert McElroy, *Grover Cleveland* (1923), I, p. 271.

4. Richardson, XI, p. 5175.

5. *Ibid.*, XII, p. 5467.

6. *Ibid.*, XII, p. 5542.

7. *Ibid.*, XII, p. 5755. Followers of the Kefauver crime investigations will note with interest that Harrison pledged support in 1890 in assisting Congress to suppress "bookmaking and pool selling in the District of Columbia." He promised to use existing laws to achieve the prohibition and explained the veto of a congressional bill because he felt that "it did not prohibit but in fact licensed what it purported to prohibit." *Ibid.*, XII, p. 5551.

8. *Ibid.*, XIII, p. 6058. Cleveland did not intend to minimize the importance of the departmental reports by not including summations of them in the annual message text. He hastened to "earnestly invite not only the careful consideration but the severely critical scrutiny of Congress and my fellow-countrymen to the reports concerning these departmental operations. . . . I press the recommendations they contain upon the respectful attention of those charged with the duty of legislation, because I believe their adoption would promote the people's good." *Loc. cit.*

9. *Ibid.*, XIII, p. 6147.

10. "I have ventured to express myself on this subject with earnestness and plainness of speech because I can not rid myself of the belief that there lurk in the proposition for the free coinage of silver, so strongly approved and so enthusiastically advocated by a multitude of my countrymen, a serious menace to our prosperity and an insidious temptation of our people to wander from the allegiance they owe to public and private integrity." *Ibid.*, XIII, p. 6087.

11. *President and Congress* (1947), p. 187.

12. *Mr. Dooley's Philosophy* (1900), p. 103.

13. Richardson, XIII, p. 6263.

14. Theodore Roosevelt, *Autobiography* (1913), p. 389.

15. *Ibid.*, p. 306.

16. "There are certain offenders, whose criminality takes the shape of brutality and cruelty towards the weak, who need a special type of punishment. The wife-beater, for example, is inadequately punished by imprisonment; for imprisonment may often mean nothing to him, while it may cause hunger and want to the wife and children who have been the victims of his brutality. Probably some form of corporal punishment would be the most adequate way of meeting this kind of crime." Richardson, XV, p. 6905.

17. *Ibid.*, XV, p. 7097.

18. *Ibid.*, XIV, p. 6669.

19. *Ibid.*, XIV, p. 6709.

20. *Ibid.*, XIV, p. 6788.

21. *Ibid.*, XIV, p. 6791. "There can be no offense heavier than that of him in whom such a sacred trust has been reposed, who sells it for his own gain and enrichment; and no less heavy is the offense of the bribe giver. He is worse than a thief, for the thief robs the individual, while the corrupt official plunders an entire city or State. He is as wicked as the murderer, for the murderer may only take one life against the law, while the corrupt official and the man who corrupts the official alike aim at the assassination of the commonwealth itself. Government of the people, by the people, for the people will perish from the face of the earth if bribery is tolerated. The givers and takers of bribes stand on an evil preeminence of infamy."

22. *Ibid.*, XV, p. 6898.

23. Roosevelt's recommendation of strict supervision and regulation of trusts was tempered by a warning that "The mechanism of modern business is so delicate that extreme care must be taken not to interfere with it in a spirit of rashness and ignorance." *Ibid.*, XIV, p. 6647. Mr. Dooley was inspired to paraphrase this section of the annual message: " 'Th' trusts are heejous monsthers built up be th' enlightened interprise iv th' men that have done so much to advance progress in our beloved country,' he [Roosevelt] says. 'On wan hand I wud stamp them undher fut; on th' other hand not so fast.' " Peter Finley Dunne quoted in Foster R. Dulles, *Twentieth Century America* (1945), p. 92.

24. Richardson, XV, pp. 7065-7066. The following citations are representative of multitudinous observations and recommendations: "History may be safely challenged to show a single instance in which a masterful race such as ours, . . . have behaved to its inhabitants with the disinterested zeal for their progress that our people have shown in the Philippines." (*Ibid.*, XIV, p. 6661); "The formation of the international tribunal which sits at the Hague is an event of good omen from which great consequences for the welfare of all mankind may flow." (*Ibid.*, XIV, p. 6718); "The course of events has shown that this canal [Panama] can not be built by private enterprise, or by any other nation than our own; therefore it must be built by the United States." (*Ibid.*, XIV, p. 6814); "Our aim should be from time to time to take such steps as may be possible toward creating something like an organization of the civilized nations." (*Ibid.*, XV, p. 6993); "I again recommend that American citizenship be conferred upon the people of Puerto Rico." (*Ibid.*, XV, p. 7233).

25. *Ibid.*, XV, p. 6923.

26. *Some Presidential Interpretations of the Presidency*, pp. 173-174.

Edward S. Corwin evaluating the effectiveness of T.R.'s messages writes: "He retained the outworn and overgrown 'annual message,' even greatly distending it. It is true that he made the message a vehicle to Congress and the country of his legislative demands in a way not previously surpassed. Yet interlarded in a scissors and paste compilation from departmental reports that ran at times to nearly thirty thousand words, these naturally failed of full effectiveness." *The President: Office and Powers*, p. 268.

27. *Our Chief Magistrate*, pp. 139-140.

28. Message I dealt with the Anti-Trust Statute; Message II with foreign

relations; Message III with a Tariff Board Report; and Message IV with all the other departments.

29. December 6, 1911.

30. Foster R. Dulles, *Twentieth Century America*, p. 113.

31. An abbreviated listing of the topic headings in Taft's second annual message provides an idea of what subjects were commanding presidential attention in 1910: Arbitration, Peace Commission, Tariff Negotiations, Fostering Foreign Trade, Aid to Our Foreign Merchant Marine, Federal Protection to Aliens, Merit System for Diplomatic and Consular Service, Public Buildings, Payne Tariff Act, Fortifications, Panama Canal, Relief of Supreme Court from Unnecessary Appeals, Injunction Bill, Postal Savings Banks, Franking Privilege, Conservation, Alaskan Railways, National Banks, Bureau of Light-Houses, Coast and Geodetic Survey, Eight-Hour Law, Workman's Compensation, Bureau of Health, District of Columbia, Freedman's Bank, Civil Service Commission, Interstate Commerce Commission, Valuation of Railroads, etc. Richardson, XVI, pp. 7492-7555.

32. *Ibid.,* XII, p. 5744.

33. *Ibid.,* XI, p. 5361.

34. *Ibid.,* XV, p. 7229.

35. *Ibid.,* XV, pp. 7230-7231. His pronouncements were seasoned by many similar references: espousal of the "White Man's burden" (XIV, p. 6661); the admonition that "each man must remember also that he is indeed his brother's keeper" (XIV, p. 6651); the belief that "The Golden Rule should be, and as the world grows in morality it will be, the guiding rule of conduct among nations as among individuals" (XV, p. 6994); and a constant reminder that "It should be our steady aim to raise the ethical standard of national action just as we strive to raise the ethical standard of individual action" (XV, p. 7053).

36. *Ibid.,* XIII, p. 6368.

CHAPTER SIX

1. *The President of the United States* (1916) p. 64. Earlier in the lecture series Wilson had said: "The President is at liberty, both in law and conscience to be as big a man as he can. His capacity will set the limit; and if Congress be overborne by him, it will be no fault of the makers of the Constitution—it will be from no lack of constitutional powers on its part, but only because the President has the nation behind him, and Congress has not." pp. 43-44.

2. Edward S. Corwin, *The President: Office and Powers*, p. 268.

3. Letter to A. Mitchell Palmer, quoted in Henry J. Ford, *Woodrow Wilson* (1916), appendix.

4. *New York Times,* April 8, 1913.

5. *The State* (1889), p. 566.

6. *The President of the United States*, pp. 48-49.

7. *Ibid.,* pp. 53-54.

8. David F. Houston, *Eight Years with Wilson's Cabinet* (1926), I, p. 52.

9. April 8, 1913.

10. April 9, 1913. The report continued, "There was plenty of color, however, in the galleries, where the dresses of the women spectators, mostly the wives and daughters of the Senators and Representatives, made a riot of color,

with blue in all of its shades predominating." Wilson was dressed in a black frockcoat and light trousers with four-in-hand grey cravat.

11. Richardson, XVII p. 7871.

12. "There was nothing about him to denote that he was ill at ease, and in fact, throughout the reading of the address, there was no tremor in his voice or anything to show that he regarded the situation as anything to be worried about." April 9, 1913.

Foster R. Dulles said of Wilson, "His vocation was teaching, but his real forte was preaching—to his students, to politicians, to the American people, to the entire world." *Twentieth Century America*, pp. 128-129.

13. April 9, 1913.

14. William Howard Taft, *The Presidency*, p. 35.

15. "The President as Chief Legislator," *Annals of the American Academy of Political and Social Science*, 307, Sept. 1956, p. 95.

16. Richardson, XVII, p. 7906.

17. *Ibid.*, XVII, p. 8015.

18. *Ibid.*, XVIII, p. 8399.

19. *Ibid.*, XVIII, p. 8637.

20. *Ibid.*, XVIII, p. 8810.

21. *Ibid.*, XVIII, p. 8022.

22. *Ibid.*, XVII, p. 8102.

23. Binkley, *President and Congress*, p. 217.

24. Richardson, (Supplement), p. 9020.

25. *Autobiography* (1929), p. 232.

26. *New York Times*, December 5, 1928.

27. Richardson (Supplement), p. 9341.

The headings in the Coolidge 1924 annual message are typical of the entire 1923-1928 series: Taxes, Waterways and Reclamation, Agriculture, Muscle Shoals, Railways, Shipping Board, National Elections, Judiciary, Prison Reform, National Police Bureau, the Wage Earner, the Negro, Civil Service and Departmental Organization, Army and Navy, Foreign Relations, Disarmament Conference and International Law, Latin America, Foreign Debts, etc. *Ibid.*, (Supplement), pp. 9454-9469.

28. *Ibid.*, (Supplement), p. 9351.

A parallel, however, was offered as early as 1899 in the same area of legislation when President McKinley reported: "The Grand Army of the Republic at its recent national encampment held in Philadelphia has brought to my attention and to that of Congress the wisdom and justice of a modification of the third section of the act of June 27, 1890, . . . " *Ibid.*, XIV, p. 6388.

29. *Presidential Government in the United States*, p. 130.

Wilfred E. Binkley writes that "Evidently, Herbert Hoover conceived it to be the President's duty to leave to Congress alone the initiation and formulation of legislation, reserving to himself merely the specific constitutional duties of recommending the fields in which legislation was needed and exercising the veto power." *President and Congress*, p. 229.

30. December 4, 1929.

31. Editorial, December 7, 1932.

32. William S. Myers, editor, *The State Papers and Other Public Writings of Herbert Hoover* (1934), II, p. 42. Cited hereafter as *Hoover Papers*.

33. *Ibid.*, II, p. 52.

34. *Ibid.*, II, p. 504.

35. *The American Presidency* (1948), p. 132.

36. *New York Times*, December 5, 1917.

37. December 6, 1923.

38. *New York Times*, December 7, 1923.

39. Richardson, (Supplement) p. 9455.

40. Editorial, December 9, 1931.

41. Wilson's style is suggested by this passage from his final annual message: "When I addressed myself to performing the duty laid upon the President . . . to present . . . an annual report . . . I found my thoughts dominated by an immortal sentence of Abraham Lincoln's—'let us have faith that right makes might, and in that faith let us dare to do our duty as we understand it'—a sentence immortal because it embodies in a form of utter simplicity and purity the essential faith of the nation, the faith in which it was conceived, and the faith in which it has grown to glory and power. With that faith and the birth of a nation founded upon it came the hope into the world that a new order would prevail throughout the affairs of mankind, an order in which reason and right would take precedence over covetousness and force; and I believe that I express the wish and purpose of every thoughtful American when I say that this sentence marks for us in the plainest manner the part we should play alike in the arrangement of our domestic affairs and in our exercise of influence upon the affairs of the world." Richardson, (Supplement) pp. 8881-8882.

42. *Ibid.*, XVII, p. 8020.

43. *Ibid.*, (Supplement), p. 9454.

44. Reported in *New York Times*, December 8, 1926.

45. Editorial, December 7, 1927.

46. *Hoover Papers*, I, p. 138.

47. *Ibid.*, I, p. 429.

48. *Ibid.*, II, p. 41.

49. Coolidge's 1925 message provides a typical example of his religious thanksgiving: "We shall not be able to gain these ends merely by our own actions. If they come at all, it will be because we are willing to work in harmony with the abiding purpose of a Divine Providence."

50. *The Course of American Democratic Thought* (1940), p. 368.

51. Richardson, XVIII, pp. 8405-8406.

52. *New York Times*, December 2, 1919.

CHAPTER SEVEN

1. Samuel I. Rosenman, editor, *The Public Papers and Addresses of Franklin D. Roosevelt* (1945), II, p. 15. Cited hereafter as *Roosevelt Papers*.

2. Dennis W. Brogan, *The Era of Franklin D. Roosevelt* (1950), p. 1.

3. Quoted, a week after his election, in *New York Times*, November 13, 1932, section 8.

4. *Roosevelt: The Lion and the Fox* (1956), pp. 197-198.

5. *Roosevelt Papers*, II, pp. 59-60.

6. *Ibid.*, III, p. 8.

7. *Ibid.*, III, p. 14.

8. *Ibid.*, IV, p. 17.

9. *Ibid.*, IV, p. 132.

10. *New York Times* reported the "press as almost united in agreeing the Roosevelt message was political and unique." N.B.C. allowed the Republicans equal radio time to make a reply; C.B.S. rejected the request. January 5, 1936. The only other President to address a night joint session of Congress was Wilson who did so in April, 1917 when he read his historic war message.

11. *New York Times,* January 5, 1936.

12. *Roosevelt Papers,* V, p. 634.

13. The President's opening remarks in 1940 explained the shift: "As the Congress reassembles, the impact of the war abroad makes it natural to approach 'the state of the union' through a discussion of foreign affairs. But it is important that those who hear and read this message should in no way confuse that approach with any thought that our Government is abandoning, or even overlooking, the great significance of its domestic policies." *Ibid.*, IX, p. 1.

14. January 8, 1943.

15. *Roosevelt Papers,* XIII, p. 43. The President told his radio audience: " . . . like a great many of my fellow countrymen, I have had the 'flu' and, though I am practically recovered, my doctor simply would not permit me to leave the White House and go up to the Capitol."

16. Press Conference Report No. 987, January 5, 1945.

17. Samuel I. Rosenman, *Working With Roosevelt* (1952), p. 511.

18. Louis Brownlow, *The President and the Presidency* (1949), pp. 69-70.

19. Burns, *op. cit.*, p. 476.

20. *Roosevelt Papers,* III, pp. 13-14.

21. *Ibid.*, V, p. 9.

22. *Ibid.*, VII, p. 14.

23. January 7, 1941.

24. *Roosevelt Papers,* IX, p. 666.

25. *Ibid.*, XI, p. 35.

26. *Ibid.*, XI, p. 39.

27. Rosenman, *op. cit.*, p. 366.

28. *Roosevelt Papers,* XII, p. 34.

29. *Ibid.*, XIII, p. 41.

30. *Ibid.*, XIII, pp. 506-507.

31. Jonathan Daniels, *The Man of Independence* (1950), p. 258.

32. *Ibid.*, p. 295.

33. *New York Times,* January 4, 1946.

34. *Ibid.*, January 17, 1946.

35. January 22, 1946.

36. Harry Truman, *Memoirs* (1955), II, p. 173.

37. Speech reported in *New York Times,* May 9, 1954. Truman also said: "Having been in these two branches of government, legislative and executive, I think I am expressing a considered and impartial opinion in saying that the powers of the President are much more difficult to exercise and to preserve from encroachment than those of the Congress . . . . upon the President falls the responsibility of obtaining action, timely and adequate to meet the nation's needs."

38. *New York Times,* January 8, 1948.

39. Editorial, *Ibid.*, January 10, 1952.

40. Eighty-third Congress, 1st session, House of Rep., document No. 1.

41. Eightieth Congress, 1st session, House of Rep., document No. 1.

42. Eighty-second Congress, 1st session, House of Rep., document No. 269.

43. Eighty-third Congress, 1st session, House of Rep., document No. 1. Truman's insistence on devoting so much of his message to an examination of the Russian system to illustrate the dimensions of its challenge, evoked the caustic comment from the House Republican majority leader that "It seems to me the message was more a message on the State of th Soviet Union than an appraisal of our situation here at home." Quoted in *New York Times*, January 8, 1953.

44. *New York Times*, section 4, July 18, 1952.

45. James Reston in the *New York Times*, section 4, November 1, 1953.

46. *New York Times*, July 25, 1954.

47. Quoted in Clinton Rossiter, *The American Presidency* (1956), p. 85. Cabell Phillips wrote in the *New York Times*, January 5, 1958: "In the past President Eisenhower has exhibited a sort of take-it-or-leave-it attitude with respect to his legislative program. He has operated on the theory that the President's function was to propose; that the decision of whether his proposals were to be enacted into law, and in what form, was the prerogative of Congress." Eisenhower was quoted from a 1957 Press Conference: "I, as you know, never employ threats. I never try to hold up clubs of any kind. I just say, 'This is what I believe to be best for the United States' and I try to convince people by the logic of my position."

Marquis Childs writing in 1958 felt that the powers of the presidency under Eisenhower had been greatly diminished: "For his failure to use the powers of the office, Eisenhower, in the interpretation of weak and strong, must be put down as a weak president. But any assessment has also to take into account the fact that he brought to the office so little preparation for what is surely the most difficult and demanding position in the world today." *Eisenhower: Captive Hero* (1958), p. 292.

48. *The President: Office and Powers*, pp. 301-302.

49. Eighty-third Congress, 1st session, House of Rep., document No. 75. *New York Times* reported: "To the home audience the President smartly attired in a grey flannel suit, pale blue shirt and darker blue tie, showed to advantage on TV screens." February 3, 1953.

50. F.D.R.'s longest address took 48 minutes, in 1938; his shortest was 22 minutes, in 1934; the average was between 30-40 minutes. His longest written message was around 8,000 words, in 1945; the average length of all his annual messages was around 4,000 words each. Truman's longest address took 50 minutes in 1947 and most of his oral messages ran between 40-45 minutes each. His final written message was around 10,000 words; the average length for all his annual reports (excluding the combination one of 1946) was around 6,000 words each.

51. Robert J. Donovan, *Eisenhower: The Inside Story* (1956), p. 313.

52. *Ibid.*, pp. 375-376.

53. *New York Herald Tribune*, January 11, 1957.

54. "Early Presidents of the United States could often fulfill the Constitutional requirements of giving to 'the Congress information of the State of the Union' in a few hundred words. The Union in the early days, and even quite

recently, has had fairly simple problems so far as the Federal Government was concerned.

"Those days are gone forever. As President Eisenhower has been finding out, the President today must not only give information and recommend 'such measures as he shall judge necessary and convenient' but he must do this in a flood of words and with the aid of a little army of experts, secretaries and advisers. Last week's State of the Union message in its original form must have been the equivalent of a medium-sized book. Even when it was delivered it was 7,000 words long. But this is just the beginning. Ahead of President Eisenhower now lie seven other messages, beginning tomorrow and running through January 28. He must give Congress his ideas on labor legislation, on social security, on a health program, on a housing program. He must produce a budget message in which recommendations as to taxation will be made. He must transmit the annual Economic Report.

"This is not all. He is expected to send special messages on foreign aid, general economic conditions and a proposed treaty of mutual security with Korea. These messages, with supporting documents, will add up to a few more volumes." Editorial, section 4, January 10, 1954.

55. December 23, 1957.

56. January 10, 1958.

57. *New York Times*, January 10, 1959.

58. Eighty-third Congress, 1st session, House of Rep., document No. 75.

59. Eighty-third Congress, 2nd session, House of Rep., document No. 251. The message was divided into three major sections: *Foreign Affairs, Strong Economy*, and *Human Problems*. The subject areas consisted of: Foreign Assistance and Trade, Atomic Energy Proposal, Defense, Internal Security, the Budget, Taxes, Agriculture, Conservation, National Highways, Post Office, Labor and Welfare, Health, Education, Housing, Veterans' Administration, and Suffrage.

60. January 8, 1954.

61. Eighty-fourth Congress, 1st session, House of Rep., document No. 1.

62. *New York Times*, section 4, January 8, 1956.

63. Section 4, January 13, 1957.

64. *New York Times*, January 6, 1956.

65. Eighty-sixth Congress, 1st session, House of Rep., document No. 1.

66. Eighty-third Congress, 1st session, House of Rep., document No. 1.

67. *Roosevelt Papers*, IX, p. 672.

68. Joseph Schiffman, "Observations on Roosevelt's Literary Style," *The Quarterly Journal of Speech*, XXXV, No. 2, April, 1949.

69. *Roosevelt Papers*, V, pp. 15-16.

70. Quoted in Schiffman, *op. cit.*, p. 225.

71. Quoted in Stephen K. Bailey and Howard D. Samuel, *Congress at Work* (1952), p. 86.

72. Quoted in William Hillman, *Mr. President* (1952), p. 65. "People want to know the facts. Most everyone now has the fundamentals of education, even if all are not highly educated, and people understand things without the trimmings. People don't go to hear people make speeches for entertainment anymore. . . . What they want are facts and supporting data to prove those facts are correct, and that's all there is to it."

73. A less serious side of Eisenhower was exposed in 1955 when the President

departed from his prepared text: "Here I am certain you will permit me this morning a personal allusion. The district where I was born has been represented in this Congress for more years than he cares to remember, I suppose, by our distinguished Speaker. Today is his birthday and I want to join with the rest of you in felicitating and in wishing him many happy returns."

74. Eighty-sixth Congress, 2nd session, House of Rep., document No. 241.

75. Wilfred E. Binkley, *The Man in the White House* (1958), pp. 171-172.

76. *Roosevelt Papers*, XIII, p. 507. In 1935 F.D.R. concluded his address with the observation: "There are growing signs of this [spiritual recovery] on every hand. In the face of these spiritual impulses we are sensible of the Divine Providence to which Nations turn now, as always, for guidance and fostering care." *Ibid.*, IV, p. 25. In 1941 the President declared: "This nation has placed its destiny in the hands and hearts of its millions of free men and women; and its faith in freedom under the guidance of God." *Ibid.*, IX, p. 672.

77. Eighty-first Congress, 1st session, House of Rep., document No. 1.

78. *Roosevelt Papers*, XI, pp. 41-42.

79. Merlo J. Pusey, *Eisenhower the President* (1956), p. 109.

80. Eighty-fourth Congress, 1st session, House of Rep., document No. 1.

81. *New York Times,* January 4, 1940.

82. Eighty-first Congress, 1st session, House of Rep., document No. 1.

83. The *Post* editorial commented: "President Eisenhower's State of the Union message reflected the amiable lassitude which Ike has brought to our national life. . . . We won't turn back the clock; but neither will we wind it with haste or zeal. It was, in short, a reassuringly unbelligerent and regrettably unhistoric message. . . . We are rather a nation becalmed, ... But surely not all our dreams and visions are dead; surely 'normalcy' is not our highest hope, surely we are not just awaiting the second coming of Calvin Coolidge." January 7, 1955.

84. Eighty-sixth Congress, 2nd session, House of Rep., document No. 241.

85. *New York Times,* section 4, January 3, 1954.

86. *Ibid.,* December 16, 1954.

87. *Roosevelt Papers*, XIII, p. 506.

88. Corwin, *op. cit.,* p. 419, note 3.

89. *New York Times,* January 8, 1954.

90. Anthony Leviero's article, "Eisenhower's TV Speeches are Major Productions" supplies this background on the President's 1953 presentation: "For his report on the State of the Union the President was without make-up and he read from a typescript. Mr. Montgomery had inspected the facilities of the House chamber in advance, however, and found the lectern too low. The President's head would be inclined downward and he feared that the TV cameras slanting at him from the gallery would catch the bounce of glaring light from the President's bald pate. So a little stand was made to raise the manuscript three inches. That enabled the cameras to get more of the face and less of the pate." *New York Times,* Section 4, January 10, 1953.

91. Section 4, January 1, 1950.

CHARTER EIGHT

1. January 7, 1955.

2. Reported in Arthur M. Schlesinger, *Paths to the Present* (1949), p. 96. The

ten designated as "great" and "near great" in the order of their superior rating were: Lincoln, Washington, F. D. Roosevelt, Wilson, Jefferson, Jackson, T. Roosevelt, Cleveland, John Adams, and Polk. Truman and Eisenhower were not included for consideration.

3. *The Presidency Today* (1956), p. 65.

4. Quoted in Vernon Louis Parrington, *Main Currents in American Thought,* I, p. 289.

5. "Presidency and Legislation: Planning the President's Program," *The American Political Science Review,* XLIX, no. 4, pp. 1014-1015.

6. *Loc. cit.*

7. "National Purpose," *The New York Times,* June 20, 1960.

INDEX

155